BARRETT

BARRETT
A Street Cop Who Cared

As told by Ethel Barrett

Fleming H. Revell Company
Old Tappan, New Jersey

Scripture quotations are based on the King James Version of the Bible.

Photographs are by Gary Baker from the Johnson-Nyquist film production BARRETT.

Library of Congress Cataloging in Publication Data

Barrett, Ethel
    Barrett: a street cop who cared.

    Biographical.
    1. Barrett, Gary, Sgt. 2. Christian biography—California—Los Angeles. 3. Los Angeles—Police—Biography. I. Title.
BR1725.B347A33   248'.2'0924 [B]   78-710
ISBN 0-8007-0918-7

Copyright © 1978 by Gary Barrett
Published by Fleming H. Revell Company
All rights reserved
Printed in the United States of America

TO Frank

BARRETT

1

It was about six in the morning when the phone call came. Gary was sitting in the Watch Commander's office. It was a medium-sized room with three gray metal desks and a couple of typewriters. The walls were green to about halfway up and glass the rest of the way to the ceiling, so you could see into the hall and across it, into several rooms beyond.

There was a tacky-looking bulletin board with notices stuck in it with thumbtacks and a couple of awards posted for arrests and convictions.

Gary was sitting at a desk, and across the room was a cop who had drifted in and sat down to chat. His name was Phil, and he was a pleasant guy, affable and jolly, the kind of guy you could use on a dull night.

And, except for routine calls, it had been a dull night. Dull nights were a respite, but they were a drag. You kept thinking your watch had stopped.

And then the phone rang.

"The night is young," Gary said, picking up the receiver and forgetting that it was only an hour before he got off duty. And then, "Sergeant Barrett speaking."

The voice on the other end of the line was hysterical. "Tape-record everything I am going to say!"

Well, that was a switch. This guy had to be some kind of a nut. Gary's first impulse was to say, "Just state your business, sir," or something like that. But suddenly he remembered something.

He and Marianne had taken part of an income-tax refund check and splurged on another tape recorder. They already had one, but this was a good deal. And he had gotten from Radio Shack a little phone tap, with a suction cup that you stick on a telephone to record phone conversations. For some strange reason, Gary had taken it to work with him that night. He had it sitting right there in the office, on a chair across the room.

So his second impulse came as a surprise, even to himself. "Okay. Just a minute, sir," he said. "Hold on."

He got up, went over to where he'd put the tape recorder, unzipped the case, and took it out.

"What are you doing?" Phil said. "What's going on?"

"Some turkey wants me to record everything he's going to say, so why not? I've got this phone-tap rig. I might as well see if it works. I haven't tried it yet." He was halfway back to the desk as he said it.

"Are you crazy?"

"Well, like we said, it's been a slow, dull night." Gary plugged in the machine and stuck in a tape.

"Maybe the guy won't wait," Phil said.

Gary tore at the box of the phone-tap rig and at the same time dipped his head toward the mouthpiece of the phone he'd left lying on the desk. "Hold on a minute, sir," he said, fumbling to get the tap out of the box. "I'm setting it up. Be with you in a minute." He spit into the suction cup, picked up the phone, and zapped the cup on the end. He was feeling good, and pleased with himself, as if he were about to play a practical joke that wouldn't hurt anybody and might provide a laugh. The caller hadn't sounded desperate, or as if he were in trouble. He sounded pompous, as if he wanted to sound off. Gary winked at Phil as he said into the phone, "Go ahead, sir. You're on."

This could be fun. Phil sat forward in his chair.

"I just recently moved out of Venice," the voice said,

startling both of them. Gary had forgotten for the moment, but the unique thing about this particular recorder and phone-tap system was that what was being taped came out the speaker; it was like a little P.A. system. They grinned at each other, and Gary said in the phone, "Okay."

"I am at 11340 Exchange Street."

Gary scribbled it down hastily.

"The phone number is five-five-five-one-two-one-two," the voice went on.

"Okay," Gary said as he wrote. "This is being recorded, so you can go ahead."

"Have you got this down, now? The phone number is five-five-five-one-two-one-two. My name is Kenneth Edward Hermin." He gave it formally, as if it were being announced from a platform, and there should be fanfare. "And it's my birthday. I'm twenty-eight years old."

"Got it," Gary said. "Happy birthday."

"I'm twenty-eight years old. And today, for the first time in my life, I've become a man in the eyes of the Lord. That's the only religious statement I'm gonna make today. Now . . . ." He said it as a pronouncement and followed it with a dramatic pause.

"I'm with you, sir," Gary said matter-of-factly.

"I'll cut it short. All I can say is I want those cars here, because you're saving a girl's life with those cars. I want my Uncle Charles Hermin to walk in with a cop. If I don't see my Uncle Charles Hermin with a cop, I don't . . . . Listen, sir, I don't . . . ."

Phil's head came up suddenly and Gary's hand tightened on the phone. "Wait a minute," he said, "are you going to try to commit suicide or something?"

"I am not, sir. This is not a suicide threat. It's a life attempt. A *life* attempt. If my Uncle Charles doesn't walk in with the first cop, this young lady is going to meet her Maker."

Phil was sitting bolt upright now. Gary shoved the address he had scribbled toward him, and he bolted out of the door. "Do you have somebody there you're holding captive?" Gary said.

Two officers had popped in out of nowhere, and were standing, listening.

"I have a captive, sir. And she's on her knees right now. And she is alive. Hold on a second." His voice faded. There was a frustrating exchange of words they could not hear. Then his voice came back strong. "Hang on, Officer."

An officer stuck his head in the doorway and nodded to Gary. "They have a car on the way now?" Gary asked. The officer nodded again.

"Mr. Hermin?" Gary said into the phone.

"Did you hear what he said, sir?" It was a girl's voice now on the phone. "He said he does have a gun," she said, her voice shaking. "And he does."

"Okay," Gary said. His voice became very quiet.

"He's not kidding—" And then she was shut off, and Hermin's voice came back.

"Officer . . . ."

"Your name is Kenneth Hermin?" Gary said. *Stall.*

"My name is Kenneth Edward Hermin."

"And what was that address?" *Stall.*

Hermin gave it again.

"Where is that?" *Stall.*

"It is in Van Nuys. You take the first street east of the freeway . . . ."

There were ten cops in the room now, curious, alert.

"Hold it! Hold—it—right—there!" The voice was off-mike, now. He was screaming at someone else. Then he came back to the phone. "Officer?"

"Yes, I can hear you," Gary said quietly.

The office was full. The corny phone-tap rig that had started out to be a lark was turning out to be like one of those old radio dramas, and everybody came in to listen! There were twenty or thirty of them now. The only sounds that could be heard were Gary's voice and the voice on the phone.

"Officer!"

"I can hear you, Mr. Hermin."

"Get my Uncle Charley here, Officer. Or else it's all over for this young lady."

A thread of excitement and apprehension shot up Gary's spine. This guy sounded spaced out. But was he bluffing? Did he really have a gun?

Hermin answered the unspoken question. "I have her covered, Officer. You had better get my Uncle Charley in here. Then I will put this gun down. And I will walk out with him."

Hermin had a curious habit of ignoring most contractions, Gary thought irrelevantly. He spoke as if they had never been invented.

"We'll get your Uncle Charley," Gary said into the phone.

"I'll tell you where he is at," Hermin said. He gave the address, several officers scribbled it hurriedly, and one of them left the room.

"Mr. Hermin, we have several cars on the way . . . ."

"I am perfectly covered right now. And the first man who comes in . . . ."

"I know that."

"I've got my single—I have got my *double*-action thirty-eight."

"All right," Gary said quietly, but his blood pressure was mounting. "Who do you have there?"

"I—have—got—my—double-action—thirty-eight." Hermin's voice rose and he spaced his words. "I'm banging it on the desk." He said it again, emphasizing each word with a thump.

"Who do you have there, Mr. Hermin?"

"I have got an employee of the studio covered."

"Mr. Hermin . . . ."

"This is a recording studio. And I've got her covered. And nobody can cover me, without killing this kid."

What had started out to be a routine call had turned into a tense drama. And incredibly, Gary was getting it on tape. The Watch Commander's office was filled with cops, all staring at him. Until a higher authority came on duty, he was in charge.

He was in charge.

Then he remembered, with a sinking feeling, that his captain would not be in until late. Captain Judd was speaking at a breakfast this morning.

Hermin had gone off on a rampage of screaming. It blared from the miniature P.A. system, mushing the mike, incoherent.

The roomful of officers listened, some impassive, a few of them boggle-eyed. There were a few rookies there. Gary could tell the seasoned officers from the rookies. It wasn't anything you could put your finger on. You could just tell who'd been in fifteen years, ten years, or one year—or who had just come in.

He knew.

He'd been a rookie once himself.

2

Being a rookie cop is not any more harrowing than being a rookie anything, except that your mistakes could be slightly more costly, like losing your life. This possibility you could minimize if you could do under fire what you learned to do so well at the police academy.

Gary Barrett started his first day with the Los Angeles Police Department determined to be the best cop in the West Valley Division. He had just graduated from the police academy two days earlier, and was awash with high ideals and a sense of mission. He was out to protect and to serve, to crush crime and make Los Angeles safe.

He drove into the parking lot of the West Valley station, found a place to park his VW, and got out, his heart pounding. The way his life had been ordered, he should have been immune to the new and the strange. He and his kid brother Steve had changed schools so often he'd lost count. His father had been a multi-talented man, who could speak with a mellifluous radio voice that announced symphonies and sports with equal facility. He could also sculpt, paint, draw, figure the most intricate math problems with ease, and do just about anything, in fact, except stay in one place.

But this was more than just a move, Gary thought as he fished for his all-too-new uniform and accoutrements. This was a whole new way of life.

He had suffered the rigors of the police academy. He had run around the track until he had dropped or vomited or both. He had done interminable push-ups and sit-ups, practiced and perfected holds and captures, shot at paper men. He had put in hundreds of hours studying criminal law, psychology, arrest procedures, radio communications, penal and vehicle codes. It was a cinch that if you were going to protect and serve, you had better learn to endure and survive.

He walked into the station, painfully aware of his fresh crew cut and new clothes, and that one of his shoes squeaked, and looked around, hoping to see a familiar face, someone from the academy, a rookie like himself. There was no one.

He asked a desk officer where the locker room was, and started down the hall in the direction the officer had pointed. First he smelled the coffee and heard the laughter, and halfway down the hall he saw the coffee room and several officers sitting around. His desire to get into the locker room and change was strong, but his desire for coffee was stronger, and it drove him into the room.

"Hi," he said, and knew intuitively that his name did not matter. He poured himself a cup and thought of sitting, then thought better of it, and stood and grinned what he hoped was a knowing and seasoned grin.

"What's your serial number?" one of the older ones said.

"Eleven-five-eighty-two," he responded promptly, automatically, wondering how, at this moment, he could even remember it.

They all burst into laughter.

He might have felt shot down, but it was good laughter, jovial, friendly, and inclusive. It rumbled up from their bellies and filled the room, and there was a warmth in it, he thought, as he tested his coffee.

"What's so funny?" he said at last, when they were through.

"It sounds like the national debt, Sonny," one of them said, and they all laughed again.

The serial numbers of some of those guys were way down in the three thousand series. You could tell how long a cop had been on the job by his number. And no one else ever got your number; you died with it. Your serial number told a lot more about you than your name.

They went back to their talk, and he gulped down the last of his coffee and headed for the locker room. He put on his uniform and felt both resplendent and foolish. He checked his accoutrements: flashlight, stick, handcuffs, gun. Then he stood before a mirror and checked himself.

Thick brown hair, prematurely laced with gray. Blue eyes, thick brows, and an in-between nose—not the noble nose of his father, and not the pug nose of his mother. A good mouth, with full lips and even white teeth. He'd grown a moustache that partly covered the upper lip and somehow seemed to make his face mean. Was his face mean, he wondered. Yes, when he squinted, he decided it could be. Well, he could stop squinting, he thought, as he brushed some lint from his uniform.

He had tried the uniform on for Marianne that morning at home, and they had embraced, getting as close as possible.

"You're big with child," he'd said. "You're bigger than you were yesterday."

And she'd answered, "Just a few weeks more."

He'd looked at her with a sudden rush of tenderness, remembering the past few months, when each morning she'd ironed his uniform for the day, three neat pleats down the back and two down the front, and each night he'd come home drawn and exhausted and unable to keep anything down, had tumbled into bed like a zombie, remembering he'd not asked Marianne how she was feeling, and falling asleep before he could get the words out.

He checked again, flashlight, stick, handcuffs, gun. Oh, yes, and notebook and pencil for roll call, he thought, fishing through his stuff.

A few minutes later he walked into the roll-call room and sat down in a chair in the back, thinking to make himself inconspicuous. The real hotshots probably sat in front.

"You're going to have to move, kid." It took a few seconds for him to realize the voice was addressing him. He turned and looked up at a veteran cop, with a face filled with a cigar and a head like a wrinkled bullet. "You're going to have to move," the face said again. "That's my seat."

Gary got up and nodded, and without a word, took another seat in the back.

More officers filed into the room. Gary stared straight ahead, but he saw the one approaching him through his peripheral vision and was prepared, this time, for the voice.

"You've got to sit over there," it said, but he was already halfway out of his seat. The third time it happened, Gary got out of his seat automatically when he saw the officer coming. He found a seat, this time toward the front of the room, knowing now that it was the old-timers who took the backseats at roll call.

He listened, trying to remember the names he heard, and when his name came, he answered, "Here." It meant more to him than the fact that he was present in the room. He was *here;* a cop at last. Only a rookie, but he was a member of the LAPD, recognized as the best police force in the United States.

When the partner assignments were called out, along with the car assignments, he hoped fervently that he would not be assigned with any of the officers whose seats he had inadvertently taken—especially the cigarface with the head like a wrinkled bullet—and was relieved when his name was called along with someone named Powers. The officer who nodded to him from across the room was a guy he'd never seen before.

After roll call was over, they crossed the room toward each other and shook hands and exchanged names. A few minutes later Gary was headed west on Vanowen, astonished to find himself in the driver's seat. He hadn't expected it, but Powers said, "You drive, kid. I'll give you directions. Know these streets?"

"No," Gary said. "Not at all."

Powers pulled a map out of the glove compartment and threw it on the seat between them. "Left down here, then pull up in front of the liquor store."

When they had stopped, Powers got out of the car. "I'll be a few minutes," he said, bending over to peer in the open window. "Keep your ear open for our calls. We're ten-A-sixty-one, remember. Give the horn one blast if we get a routine call. For a Code Two (get there, but no red lights or siren), two blasts. If we get a Code Three (emergency, red lights and siren), three blasts and I'll come running. Got it?"

Gary nodded, and Powers turned and went on into the liquor store. Gary could see him through the window, talking to the manager. The radio squawked on endlessly, but there was no action on the air, and after what seemed like hours, but was actually twenty minutes, Powers came out and got into the car with no explanations.

Thirty minutes later, they pulled up to a pay phone.

Powers got out again and talked endlessly on the phone, while again Gary waited, listening for calls.

"Married, kid?" Powers asked, when they were finally driving along again. Gary told him yes without elaborating. Maybe Powers was having marital problems, he thought. Maybe that's what all the phoning was about. But it turned out that Powers was single and the phone calls concerned a new outside business venture, and he had just negotiated a big sale, his first.

"Pull up here, kid," Powers interrupted his thoughts. He pulled up to the curb again and stifled a groan. Powers got out without a word and disappeared into a deli.

Gary sat in the car and stewed. His uniform was beginning to itch in the heat of the ninety-degree weather. October was one of the hottest months of the year in Los Angeles. He thought of Marianne at home, how he had told her, when he'd left for this first adventurous day, that he was going out to crush crime. They'd both smiled, him a little grimly, for he'd been nervous.

He had met Marianne at Forest Home, a huge Christian conference grounds in the San Bernardino mountains. In talking, they had discovered that they'd really met fifteen years before, at a Christian conference ground in New York, where her father, Dr. McBain, had been speaking. Gary, who was then six, had thrown rocks into the duck pond, and Marianne, who was four, had watched him with fear and trepidation. At Forest Home they had both laughed about their earlier meeting, surprised at the coincidence.

Marianne had grown into a beauty. She had a mop of curly, dark brown hair, a face to be remembered, brown eyes, a splendid nose, full wide lips, and even white teeth and a smile that could knock you over and a figure that could send you spinning if you didn't keep your head. She was also about five foot seven, and Gary observed that with heels she could give a guy a little trouble.

In the days and weeks that followed, Gary's defense mechanism had gone into high gear. He had run for a while, taking out other girls, hurling himself out of her life, but like a boomerang, he had always come back. And in the end, he had not been able to run. He had asked her father for her hand, which was a melodramatic piece of business when you read about it, he thought, but pretty grim business when you actually did it.

They had been married the day after Thanksgiving, by her father, in her father's church. It had been beautiful, all candlelight and autumn flowers, with his mother fighting tears and her mother stolid and composed. They'd gone off on a honeymoon to San Francisco, and after that there had never been, not ever, not for one moment, any other woman for him.

He thought of her, waiting at home for him, and of how he'd hoped to regale her with laughter or move her to tears with all his tales of derring-do, and he fumed in a welter of sweat and frustration. He was five hours into this shift, and he'd spent most of them stewing in a parked car.

He thought of giving the horn three blasts that would make Powers leave the floor a couple of feet beneath him and come running. Though he did not dare do it, he chuckled at the thought.

Then another thought occurred to him, and he started to get out of the car. He knew he shouldn't do it, even while he was walking toward the store where Powers was holding court, but he opened the door and went into the store and felt the immediate and immense relief of air conditioning.

"A car just drove by, going pretty fast, and I think we ought to chase it down, don't you?" he said. Powers fixed him with a baleful gaze, and Gary realized in the silence that his heart was pounding and his carotid arteries felt swollen. He wondered if they showed, pulsing there up the sides of his neck. Powers and the store proprietor exchanged glances, and then, unexpectedly, Powers turned back to Gary and said, "Okay, kid. Let's go."

They went back to the car without a word.

"Go straight. And slow. I'll tell you when to turn," Powers said, not mentioning the speeding car that both of them knew didn't exist.

From there on, things picked up. Powers, it turned out, had a sixth sense when it came to spotting errant drivers, even when to Gary they seemed to be driving normally. They pulled over one car, ran the driver over the air, and he came back with $347 worth of warrants, a bonanza. Powers had street savvy too, and an easy low-keyed way about him with a suspect.

The rest of the shift went quickly, and though it had not been filled with derring-do, it had been productive, finally, and Gary felt that he had learned something. Powers really was a canny and competent cop, but Gary was glad to have a senior partner who had some human frailties, too, and that they were ordinary ones.

3

The atmosphere in the Watch Commander's office had suddenly gone tense.

Up to that moment, the mood had been one of excitement, and in some perverse sort of way, entertaining—quite possibly because it was coming out of the P.A. system Gary had set up, and had an air of unreality about it, like a play. And possibly because, like many violent men, Ken Hermin could be quite charming. Gary had chatted back and forth with him, also charming and affable.

"Mr. Hermin, why do you want to do that?" Gary said into the phone, as if he were asking Hermin why he wanted to change jobs or break his dental appointment.

"I want to do this so I can get out of here with my life," Hermin said. "And I'm not leaving till I see my Uncle Charley . . . ." He began to ramble again.

"Did she threaten you, sir?" Gary interrupted, nudging him back on the track.

"Who?"

"The person you have covered."

"I have—listen man—" Hermin cleared his throat, the way some people do before they say something they think is very important. "I—am—not—nuts. I want Uncle Charley here. And I want my girl here. Her name is Edith, Miss Edith Randall."

The attention in the room heightened, heads jerked up. This could mean more trouble, or more time to stall, depending on how hard the girl would be to find. Gary pressed the mouthpiece of the phone against his chest and picked up his pencil, at the same time nodding to one of the officers in the room. "You just volunteered," he said, his voice barely audible, then turned back to the phone, "What's her number?"

Hermin gave it, and Gary scribbled it down. So did the officer whom he had just volunteered, and he hurried from the room as the others backed away to make a path for him.

"Officer? I want you to hear me real good. You're gonna save a girl's life by bringing the lady that—I—love," Hermin said, slowing down on the last three words, with tones so dulcet they would have done well on a talking Valentine.

"We'll get your girl," Gary said, "and your Uncle Charley."

"Okay. I want my Uncle Charley, too." And then, suddenly, "Do not open that mail slot, or this gal is dead! This gal is real dead!" It was a scream, so loud it was mushing the mike. There was an air of palpable tension in the room. More officers crowded in, attracted by the noise. "I checked the security in this building, and I know I am covered," Hermin went on. "I've got it covered!"

Gary put the phone against his chest again. "Our units are there," he said. "Get on the air. Tell them to quit playing with that mail slot. And tell them to check for another phone there, maybe a pay phone. And get a line established in here, so we can find out what's going on." He went back to the phone.

"You and I are friends," Hermin came back. "But I've been so wired for ten days that I didn't know if I was coming or going."

So the guy was spaced out. Violent by nature or not, he was violent now.

"Hey listen," Gary interrupted, glad that he was still capable of easy chatter, "I don't want to see anything happen to this girl, because—"

"This girl is with the Lord, Officer. She has told me so. And she has strayed. We are not blaming anybody in the world, Officer. We're blaming mankind's basic greed. That is all I'm saying. We're not blaming any race, religion, or creed for so many ills of the American society."

Good grief. One of those.

There was a hubbub in the room now, not of inattention, but of action—officers volunteering, hushed reports. The room was stifling as more crowded in. Those coming on duty wanted to know what was going on, the rest, off duty, were reluctant to leave.

Gary heard it only dimly. He was beginning to feel, unaccountably, a vague sort of identification with this voice. It's like he's screaming in the dark, Gary thought, and suspected that was trite and schmaltzy even before he finished thinking it. Still, there was that listen-to-what-I'm-not-saying feeling about the guy.

"Are you a religious man, Mr. Hermin?" he heard himself saying.

"I have become a religious man on my birthday, Officer," came back quickly—too quickly.

"What is your faith?" Gary asked.

"My . . . I'm . . . I was born a Jew."

"What is your faith now?"

"I am a Christian at heart. *I—am—a—Christian—at—heart.*" He had a habit of repeating anything he thought important, spacing his words dramatically.

Don't let him off that easily, Gary thought. "Do you believe that Christ died for your sin?" he asked.

There was a pause, the sense of nonplus that always seemed to follow that question. "Do you believe in the blood of Christ?" Gary persisted.

Hermin had gone by the moment and had said no, by default. "I believe in Christ as a historical man, and I believe in the all-seeing power of the Lord," he answered, saying exactly nothing.

"Well, then, what exactly is your religious faith? How can you state . . . ."

"I am a Jew, sir. I am a Jew."

Gary could see he was getting nowhere. "Well, I understand that," he said. "How do you . . . ."

"Hold it!" Hermin screamed, off the phone. *"Hold it!"*

The Watch Commander's office went silent again. Gary held the phone away from his ear and looked up at the officers in the room. He held up his hand for continued silence and went back to the phone. "Mr. Hermin, why do you want to put this girl in eternity?"

"I don't, sir. I want you to help me save her life. And I've got her so covered it—is—incredible," Hermin began, and launched into what promised to be some lengthy palaver.

"Does Hays have a phone line in yet?" Gary asked, to no one in particular. Two or three officers answered at once. Hays had called in; he was on a pay phone.

"Where is it in the building?" Gary wanted to know.

"It's in the hall that runs along the side wall of the room where Hermin is."

"Did the other guys get in?"

"Yeah, he's covered. But if something goes wrong, he could kill the hostage."

"Have they contacted his uncle yet? Or the girl?"

The faces all came up negative.

Stall.

"Listen, Mr. Barrett," Hermin was saying, "I met a

A Street Cop Who Cared

man who invited me to go deer hunting up in Utah—Chris, you hold still. You just hold still—"

"I like to camp, too." *Keep him talking.* "I just went down to Mexico—"

"Hang on, Officer Barrett. Because I'm not condemning any living thing in this earth. I'm not condemning any living plant—"

"I know that."

"I've got six thirty-eight slugs, Buster."

"And we've got people on our phones, trying to contact the people you'd like to have us contact." Gary shut him off, a strident note creeping into his voice for the first time.

"Okay. Have you got those people on the phone?"

Gary looked up toward the door, hoping for someone to poke his head in and nod yes. Please, someone, poke your oh-so-beautiful, welcome head in and nod yes. Several near the door shrugged and shook their heads negatively. It was no. They couldn't be contacted—either of them.

Fortunately Hermin didn't wait for an answer. "I'm watching that mail slot real close," he shouted, away from the phone. "And if any tear gas comes in here—if tear gas comes in here—you've got a dead girl on your hands. I've got you so covered that it is sickening, Buster." Then Hermin spoke into the phone, "Listen, Officer, it's getting critical. I want to hear some sirens in a hurry. I want to hear some sirens in a big hurry."

"We're doing all we can for you."

"Chris says give 'em sirens. You hear what she says? She's kneeling here, and she says 'Give it to 'em.' "

"Mr. Hermin—" Gary began.

"Now are you gonna snuff us both?" Hermin's voice rose.

Gary pointed out the Watch Commander's office door, toward the hall. "Tell 'em to tell Hays to give them a siren," he said over Hermin's voice, "but keep it low."

"Now listen, Officer, do you want me to snuff us both?" Hermin screamed it, this time. Gary's heart squeezed down with a *thalump,* and then his blood seemed to leap through his veins with a spurt, like water after the sudden release of pressure on a garden hose.

" 'Cause it's happenin', man, it's really happenin'," Hermin was screaming now.

"We're not trying to snuff anybody. We're just trying to save this girl's life and help you out. Both."

"Listen, Officer—"

There was a pause, and they waited, silent.

Then there was a dry little click, sort of like the "tch-tch" people make with the teeth and tongue to express disapproval.

"Here comes one shot, and I've got five more. Are you ready?"

Oh, God. Oh, good God.

"Don't do it, Mr. Hermin. Don't do it. Please don't do it." Gary's voice was pleading but surprisingly calm.

"Are you ready? Are you ready? Listen. This is one shot."

"I don't want to hear it."

"You're gonna hear it, right now."

"I don't want to. Please don't. Please don't, Mr. Hermin."

But Hermin's voice came back again.

"You're—gonna—hear—it—right—now."

The room was silent. Gary steeled himself with that numb feeling you get when you've just taken a slice out of your finger and are waiting for the pain to come.

4

Gary had never gotten used to the horror of witnessing somebody's taking another human life by violence. He hoped he never would.

He'd had his first whiff of violence when he was a rookie, and then it was only that, a whiff. He had not seen it.

He was working the night shift with Danny, an oldtimer who had seventeen years of service racked up, and no scars to show for them, either physical scars or the intangible scars of the psyche.

Gary reached for a map and then remembered he did not need one. Danny had lived in the Valley all his life; he knew every street.

"The house I live in is built under a giant oak tree, must be hundreds of years old," Danny said. "Biggest tree you ever saw, all gnarled and scarred. I played under that tree when I was a kid."

"That sounds great," Gary said. "I live in Simi Valley."

"Oh, yeah, out through the Santa Susana Pass. It's new out there."

"It's a tract development. Our first house. We lived in an apartment before, in Van Nuys. This seems great by comparison. But the trees we've planted are only two feet high. I've built a fence, though, and planted a lawn, and we've got a dog, so it seems more like living."

"Any kids?"

"One. Our second."

It was Marianne's second Caesarean, and she'd gone into it gamely. When they told him his second child was a son and gave him Michael to hold, he took him fearfully, remembering Melissa.

"Our first died at six months. A daughter, Melissa," he explained. "We called her Missy."

Danny said nothing, but it was a comfortable silence, and Gary was grateful, for he did not want to talk about it.

It was then that the call came over the radio: "See the man, four-fifteen. Man in a vehicle." Danny made a U-turn, doubled back, and headed for the address. It turned out to be a quiet residential street, nice houses, and no sign of trouble. There was a car parked in front of the address, an old Chevy with Oregon plates. They pulled up behind it and parked.

"Let's go," Danny said. They got out of the car, walked up to the Chevy, looked in briefly and saw nobody, went up to the house, and rang the bell. A man answered immediately. They identified themselves, and Danny said, "What's the trouble?"

"There's a kid living in that car," the man said, "and it's been there for a week. Sometimes he's there and sometimes he's gone for hours. We haven't worried about it too much, because he hasn't caused any trouble. But tonight my wife and I are going out, and we have a baby-sitter coming, and we thought . . . . Well, I got a little worried, you know, with a baby-sitter. A young kid . . . ."

"You did right," Danny said. "We'll check it out. You and your wife have a good time tonight."

A few more questions and they went back to the car, trying the doors, and looking in, carefully this time. Sure enough, there was a man inside, sleeping in the backseat. They knocked on the window, and the man woke up, dazed at first, then, seeing that they were cops, he opened the door and got out. He was a young man—just a kid, really. And he seemed like a nice kid.

In his best Barnaby Jones voice, Danny asked for his identification, and the kid gave it politely. Then Danny took his arm and started to walk him some paces away, talking easily. He turned casually to Gary before they walked away and said softly, so only Gary could hear, "Run him."

Danny smelled something.

Gary picked up the mike and ran him, then waited, stamping his feet against the cold of the San Fernando Valley night. A male voice finally came back on the air and said, "Ten-A-sixty-one, is your subject out of range of hearing?"

Gary glanced at Danny and the kid, some distance away, talking.

"Roger," he said softly, close into the mike. "Go ahead."

"Your suspect is wanted for questioning in Oregon in regard to a homicide up there. That's all we have at this time. They just want to talk to him about it. He might have some information on a homicide."

"Anything on the car?" Gary said.

"Yeah. The description and license number you gave us are for the same car they want."

Gary said, "Roger," hung up the mike, and walked over to Danny and the kid. Danny turned his head to the side, and Gary gave him the information, in key words, almost in code, softly.

Gary had been taught all the approaches—be nice, be hard, be soft, be mean, throw people off, get them to want to talk to you.

But Danny used one Gary had never seen before.

It was the father-son routine, and the odd part was, Danny really meant it.

In the same easy voice he said, "They want to talk to you about a homicide in Oregon. I don't know anything about it, but we'll have to take you down to the station and check it out. You may have been a witness. Can you tell us anything about it?"

This was before the Miranda decision.

"Well, I worked up there," the kid said. "But I haven't any idea what you're talking about. It couldn't be me."

"You worked up there?" Danny said, and then, "D'you mind if we check out your trunk?" He was already opening the trunk as he said it, and he pawed over the clothing inside. It was all soaked with blood.

"It's chicken blood," the kid said. "I worked on a chicken farm up there, and my job was to kill chickens."

Danny was playing the father role. Gary followed suit and tried the brother role. "When I went to Hampden Du Bose Academy in Florida, one of my chores was to kill chickens. We raised our own poultry there. I killed forty chickens every Monday for years. I tallied it up one time. I figured I'd killed thirty-five thousand chickens."

Danny slammed the trunk door shut, and went on talking easily, but not about chickens, about conscience. Gary could not remember afterward what Danny said. But suddenly the kid sighed, a deep shuddering sigh that went all through him, and he seemed to crumble and fall apart slowly, like a biscuit, crumbling first at the edges and then falling apart.

"Okay," he said finally, "I'll tell you all about it."

They got into the police car silently, and Danny started back to the station.

"Want to tell us about it now?" he said.
"I borrowed some money from my boss," the kid began.
There was a long silence. Danny did not press him. There was time.
"He was mean," the kid said at last. "Mean. And when I told him I couldn't pay it yet, he got real mean."
They waited.
"The ranch—the chicken ranch—I really did work on a chicken ranch. I wasn't lying. The ranch was off in Toolyville, kind of a wooded area outside Portland. And I got desperate. Not far off, there were some trailers, and some old people living in them."
Danny said nothing. Gary followed suit and remained silent.
"There was one trailer, a little apart from the rest, and I parked there and went up and knocked on the door," the kid went on. "And a woman answered. I only wanted to ask her for some money so I could pay back my boss. But I figured I might have some trouble, so on the way to the door, I picked up a rock. She had a little garden with some rocks alongside, and I—I just picked one up, before I knocked on the door. And I held it behind my back."
Gary smelled death.
"Well, I asked her for some money, and she smelled a rat and wouldn't open the door, except only a little, not all the way. I wasn't getting anywhere, but I still had the rock in my hand. Then I asked her if I could at least have a drink, and when she hesitated, I kicked the door the rest of the way in, and went in."
They stopped for a red light and were silent.
"Well, she was a strong woman," the kid went on. "She was very strong, and she started fighting. And I

fought back all the harder. She made me desperate. She ran into the bedroom and tried to close the door. I knew I was in trouble. She might call the police in there, and I'd go to jail for going into her house. I figured I had to quiet her down.

"I kicked the bedroom door in, and she fought and scratched and screamed like a banshee. That threw me into even more of a panic. I took that rock and started hitting her alongside the head as hard as I could. And she got away from me. She ran into the bathroom, and I kicked my way in there, too, and I picked up a mirror, a four-cornered mirror, and I beat her in the head with that. And she ran back into the bedroom . . . ."

They were nearly at the station house.

"And I finished her off with the rock. I still had that rock."

"Did you rape her?" Danny asked.

There was a long silence.

And finally, "Yes."

"Before or after you finished her off with the rock?"

No answer.

They pulled into the parking lot of the station house.

Before they got out of the car, Danny turned to the kid. "How much money did you get?"

"About three or four bucks."

Lord, Gary thought, *three or four bucks*. It was enough to make you vomit.

"I got into my car and went into town. I had a charge account there at a little Western-clothing store. I charged a bunch of clothes and got back in my car and headed south. I ran out of money and out of gas right on that street where you found me. I really ran out of gas right there. I didn't even know where I was."

"How did you manage to stay there all that time without money?" Danny said, still very easy.

"I scrounged around behind stores and all over and found soda bottles to cash in and scoured garbage cans—anything I could find. I lived on garbage and candy bars."

They got out of the car in silence. Gary followed Danny and the kid into the station. They turned him over to the detectives and stood there, outside the glass, for a few moments while the detectives set up a tape recorder and started to question him. Then they left.

"It's past End-of-watch," Danny said. "Want some coffee?"

"No," Gary said. "I want to go home."

Marianne was waiting.

He told her about it as they lay in bed, as if in the release he could purge himself of the horror behind the gentle voice of Danny and the low-keyed tale told by the kid, told almost dreamlike, as if he himself could not believe it.

Long afterward, when Marianne lay on her back, sleeping quietly, he thought of Melissa. The ripping pain had come later, when he and Marianne had gone back to the grave and she had sunk to her knees and clawed at the fresh sod that had been laid over it. And that night they had lain in bed, clinging to each other in silence, like children afraid of the dark.

5

Norman Judd kissed his sleepy wife good-bye and left through the kitchen door that led to the garage of his home in Whittier. He got in his car, pressed the remote control, and the electric door of the garage swung up with a groan. He backed his car out, and a few minutes later was headed into the early freeway traffic. He was speaking at a breakfast in Van Nuys that morning.

He was a handsome man of medium height, and solidly built, with dark hair, brown eyes, and an open face that belied his years in the police department. In his uniform he looked every bit the part of Captain Norman Judd, but had his life been differently ordered, he could have been a perfect picture of the junior executive.

At the station, he drove into the space marked Commander, Van Nuys Division. It was only seven o'clock, but he wanted to get in a quiet forty minutes in his office, for he had inadvertently left his notes there, and he figured he could do himself nothing but good if he went over them before he went to the breakfast. He left his car and headed for the heavy, encased doors that led into the ground floor of the building, and unlocked his way in.

It wasn't until he had closed the door behind him that an instinct, known only to bloodhounds and some very seasoned cops, brought him up short. His sixth sense hadn't told him what it was—only that something was wrong.

Inside the Watch Commander's office, everyone was

silent, waiting. It seemed like minutes, but it was only a few seconds.

"Don't shoot, Mr. Hermin," Gary was saying. "Please don't shoot."

"Now listen, Officer," Hermin's voice came back. "You've got this on tape. I've asked you for my Uncle Charley. I've asked you for Edith Randall, the woman I love. I want them here before I walk out of here on two feet."

Keep talking, Gary thought. Keep talking and don't come up for air. For he had seen someone coming up the hall. Michael the archangel, he thought, or perhaps the angel Gabriel—but in reality, it was Captain Judd.

Captain Judd, who was supposed to be at a breakfast, but who was unaccountably and blessedly here. There was no way he could possibly be here, but here he was, coming into the room, the officers pressing back to let him through. And he was fresh shaven and showered and immaculate and cool, even on this smoggy and now all-beautiful August morning.

Gary pointed him toward Phil.

Hermin was still raving, so Gary held the phone against his chest and watched Judd and Phil conversing quietly. Then Judd came toward him. Gary held the phone up to him in a question, but Judd waved it back and shook his head, leaned against the end of the desk, picked up another phone quietly, and listened. It was so reassuring that Gary went limp. He looked up at Judd, but Judd shook his head in the negative and jabbed a finger at him to carry on.

"Mr. Hermin, would you like to talk to the commander of the Van Nuys Division?"

"I wanna hear some sirens, Officer."

Gary tried again. "I tell you what, Mr. Hermin. We

can give you some big horsepower right now, if you'd like to talk to the captain."

"I want to hear some sirens right now."

"We gave you sirens."

"They're not loud enough. I can't hear them."

"It's pretty early in the morning. You want to wake up the neighborhood?"

"I want to hear some sirens right now. I don't hear anything. And I'm giving you one minute right now by my wristwatch so I can . . . . Hey, listen, Officer Barrett . . . . So I can coordinate activities."

Now it was General Hermin speaking. Gary's shoulders sagged in frustration. Who was in charge, after all, when you were dealing with a guy swinging a loaded gun, who had an innocent hostage kneeling on the floor?

"All right," he said, suddenly weary. "We've got sergeants on the way. I'm calling communications . . . ."

"Listen, Officer Barrett, I want the sirens right now! You're gonna kill two people if you're not here fast."

Two people? Did he have another hostage?

"Who's the other one?" Gary said.

"Me."

There was a corporate sigh of relief.

"What are you going to kill yourself for?"

"Hey listen, Buster," Hermin's voice came back. "I'm gonna go easy. If there's any tear gas put in this place, I am shooting this girl next to me, and I am getting ready to fight off whoever comes in with whatever shots I've got."

Gary groaned inwardly. Hermin had every advantage.

"Mr. Hermin . . . ."

"Hey listen to me, Buster."

"I'm listening, sir." *Keep your cool. Stall.*

"I'm calling you 'Buster,' but I've got a great respect for you."

Gary tried a new tack. "Have you called your Uncle Charley yourself yet?"

"I haven't. I'm not getting off the phone with you, Buster."

Gary looked up at Judd, who looked back at him coolly, indicating that Gary was still in charge.

"Here comes the shot through the wall. Now listen. Listen to the shot through the wall."

Gary cupped the phone against his chest, looked at Judd. "Hays is on the other side of that wall," he said. "In a phone booth."

Their eyes locked.

"Here comes the shot through the wall, right now. Now listen."

"Mr. Hermin, please—"

"Listen to the shot through the wall."

"Don't do it. Come on, now—"

And then the shot.

The sound exploded out of the P.A. system, not the ping of a .25 or a .22 or even a .32; Hermin was telling the truth. He had a .38, which was a standard police weapon. The officers recoiled almost imperceptibly. It seemed to be mental more than physical. Gary's hand shot up to his face. "I heard it," he said softly.

"Listen to me, Buster, listen to me. I've got five more, and they're ready to go," Hermin said, and then repeated it, spacing his words, "They—are—ready—to—go."

Stall.

"I thought you and I were supposed to be friends."

"We are friends, Officer." And then Hermin's voice rose to a scream. "But I want out of here, right now!"

"Mr. Hermin," Gary began quietly.

"*I—want—out—of—here—right—now!*" The voice mushed the mike again. "Otherwise I'm killing this girl in thirty seconds!"

"Mr. Hermin, listen a minute." Gary looked up at Judd.

Judd spoke into his phone. "Mr. Hermin, this is Captain Judd, the commander of the Van Nuys Division."

There was a short silence, while they could feel Hermin absorbing that. Then, "Captain Judd?" he said, both surprise and suspicion in his voice.

"Yes, sir," Judd said.

"Who is the chief of police?" Hermin jumped in, so they were both talking together.

"—and I have the authority to do anything that you need, sir," Judd finished.

But Hermin wasn't giving up. "Who is the chief of the police?"

"Ed Davis," said Judd.

"Who is the second in command?"

"That depends, sir."

"Who is the chief of police in Denver?" The slight pause that followed told Hermin that he had the whip, and his attitude became swaggering now. "You'd better say it right. You'd—better—say—it—right."

"I can only take care of Van Nuys, Mr. Hermin," said Judd, in a tone indicating that he would not be intimidated.

Hermin made another try. "You say it right or you've got a dead girl on your hands."

Gary smothered a groan. To be at the mercy of some unknown voice like that wiped you out. You couldn't believe it, but the gun told you you had better believe it and keep your cool. "Mr. Hermin," he began, "don't let who a chief of police is decide . . . ."

"Hey, I can do it, Chris," Hermin said to the hostage, then back into the phone, "I want the cops here, man, and I'm holding out for blood."

It was beginning to sound like a broken record. Judd and Gary exchanged looks, and Judd tried again.

"Mr. Hermin, this is Captain Judd again. Would you tell me how we can get you out of there?"

"Hey, man, I don't wanna hear you, I wanna hear some sirens, Mister, I wanna hear some sirens pretty quick."

Judd nodded to an officer waiting by the door, and the officer disappeared.

"Hang on," said Judd into the phone. "We're going to get the sirens."

"Listen, Buster, and I wanna see the people I called for."

"They'll be there," said Judd. The sirens could be heard in the background over the P.A. "You hear the sirens?"

But Hermin, having gotten his way, was no longer interested. He was busy working on his next demand. "I wanna see the people I called for."

"You hear the sirens now, Mr. Hermin?" Judd persisted.

"I'm not gonna shoot her over that noise, I swear to Christ—"

"No, but do you hear the sirens now?" Judd was determined to keep him on the track.

"I hear them, I hear them!" Hermin shouted. "Now the next thing I want—and you're doin' it real good—the next thing I want before this young woman and I walk out of here alive—"

"You promise you'll let her walk out, sir?"

"I swear."

"What can we do for you, then, to assure ourselves that you will let her out of there alive?"

"I . . . . Okay. Do you want to hear my word?"

"I would like that."

"I heard the sirens, and I'm not gonna shoot her over the noise. I promise you, Buster. I'm not nuts, man."

"I know that."

"Hold it!"

"Mr. Hermin."

"Wait a second, Officer. I've been put up against the wall by cops a lot of times. And I know how to put someone up against the wall."

"Listen to me. Listen to me," said Gary. "Are you up against the wall now?"

"I'm on my knees, praising the Lord."

Suddenly, screaming and confusion rattled the tape recorder and made both Gary and Judd snatch their receivers away from their ears.

"I sent more cars out," Gary said to Judd. "They must be there." He made a futile attempt to get Hermin's attention. "The police are outside, eh?" he tried.

"Hold it! I swear to God! Hold it right now!"

"Mr. Hermin, listen to me. Mr. Hermin, this is Barrett. Keep talking to me—please. Don't talk to the people outside. Talk to me."

"Now listen, Officers. Wait a second. Wait—a—sec—ond!" He gave each syllable equal emphasis.

Then, suddenly, silence.

Judd and Gary looked at each other.

"Okay, Barrett." Hermin's voice was quiet. "I'm gonna slow down now. I'm gonna slow—down—real—good."

"Okay," Gary said matter-of-factly, matching the quiet voice.

"I've got a trumpet here," Hermin went on. "You know, this reminds me of the trumpet that's supposed to be from Gabriel." Then, off-mike, "Hold it now! Chris, tell 'em at the door."

They waited, trying to hear what was being said; it was too far away.

"He's got the hostage talking to the officers outside the door," Gary said. Judd nodded. Finally, Hermin's voice came back on the phone.

"Have you got the tape running, Officer?"

"I sure do," Gary said.

"If you will, please—just stay with me, Barrett. Just stay with me. You're going to keep me from dying, and you're going to keep me from killing."

"I'm with you."

"Mr. Hermin. This is Captain Judd. I—"

"Barrett, you're the only one I wanna talk to right now. You got me?"

Judd tried again. "Mr. Hermin, may I offer a suggestion?"

"Listen, don't stop me."

"Okay," said Gary.

"Okay, Buster, let's keep on going. I'm calling you Buster. But I've been called Buster . . . ."

"I've been called a lot worse," Gary said dryly.

"I've been called a lot worse by some of your brothers in uniform. I've been called a lot worse because my hair is long."

"I do that on vacations."

Hermin ignored that. He ignored anything he did not want to hear. "Are you with me, Officer?"

"Yep," Gary said, with a patience he did not feel.

"Okay. The Lord said unto man that if he would accept the Lord in his heart he would have everlasting love. That's all I'm asking for."

Somewhere, somehow, this man had heard the Gospel. And sometime, somehow, he had screwed it all up.

"The Lord also said to do unto others as you would have them do unto you," Gary answered. "It's in Matthew, chapter six."

"I'm giving a young girl who is twenty-one years old a chance to live."

Judd leaned toward Gary. "See if you can get me on," he said softly.

"Ken," Gary said. It was the first time he'd used Hermin's first name. "Will you talk to Captain Judd now?"

"When I see some faces that are familiar to me, when I see Edith's face, when I see Uncle Charley's face, coming through the glass of the reception room of this recording studio. Man, you are giving me the opportunity to get right. You've helped me get right."

"I'm glad about that," Gary said. "Listen, I've got officers on their tracks right now. But right now you're going to keep your end of the promise and let Captain Judd talk to you."

"Captain Judd, I'm willing to talk to you. I want you to hold—listen, man, I make one request. Hold all tear gas out of this building. Otherwise you'll have a dead girl on your hands. And if you send a rookie in with a shotgun, she's gone."

"Let me make another suggestion, Mr. Hermin. You seem to have a lot of confidence in Sergeant Barrett."

"I like Sergeant Barrett's voice, and he sounds like a man who has received the Lord in his heart. That's all I'm saying."

Without looking up, Gary knew everyone was looking at him. Everyone knew he was a Christian. But he felt at that moment that he'd blown it more than he'd shown it.

"Right, Mr. Hermin," Judd said. "You read him correctly."

The room was quiet.

A sudden coolness emerged under Gary's collar, and he realized it was a fresh outpouring of sweat.

"Okay, sir," Hermin said.

And suddenly Gary knew, without knowing, what was coming. No, he thought, whatever it is, no.

"Would it give you any more assurance," Judd said, "if Sergeant Barrett were out at the scene? If he came out there to talk to you?"

Gary wanted, at that moment—more than he'd ever wanted anything in his life—to go home.

6

Home was still in Simi Valley, but it was not the same. The baby trees had soared to great heights. The cedar fence that Gary had put in was covered with orange and red bougainvillea. The rose bushes they had put in had grown into a four-foot-high border along the front driveway. The peach tree they had planted was up to the roof and over, and some sprigs of ivy they had snitched from an abandoned farmhouse on one of their jaunts had completely covered the attached garage.

Marianne had gone in for her third Caesarean. Another boy. They named him Sean.

Sean was a textbook boy, very proper, very independent, very self-contained, and very disconcerting. Needing no attention, he'd gotten little. He'd integrated himself into the family, and, as if discovering that he'd have no eager and nervous sponsors, had established himself firmly and quietly with a you-give-me-no-trouble-and-I'll-give-you-none air.

"Sometimes," Marianne would say, "he spooks me."

And then Marianne had gone in for her fourth Caesarean, and the doctors had said this was the last. She'd had a bad time. But this time it was the girl she'd wanted, with a piquant face and huge brown fawnlike eyes and tiny bones. She weighed only four pounds, and Gary had been afraid to even touch her. Michelle.

It was a long while before they got out of the habit of periodically calling her Melissa by mistake, and they had to keep reminding themselves that she was herself, and had not come to take anybody else's place.

Marianne was going to church. Gary was not. He could not bring himself to, and he couldn't quite figure out why.

In Van Nuys, they'd gone to a church up in Bel Air, and he had loved it. He had joined the choir, and it was a good one. He had been happy there, and it was months before he realized that Marianne was not.

It was a church that catered to celebrities, she said quietly and evenly one night. It would have been better if she had stormed. She was constantly being asked to move by an usher, because some movie actor was coming in and they needed a seat for him. She felt like a child in the wrong place, being told to get out and make room for an adult.

When Melissa died, she phoned the church and asked if she could see the pastor. She said that it was urgent; her child had died. Someone at the other end of the phone told her perfunctorily that he was very busy. No, he could not come to the phone. No, he could not possibly see her until the following week. Was it important?

Was it important.

"My father," she had ended bitterly, "would have *made* time to at least pray with a troubled person on the phone."

She'd begged off going to church after that. And so, at last, he had dropped out, too.

After they moved to Simi Valley, Marianne began to take the children to Sunday school and to go back to church herself, but she went alone. Gary made no excuses. He just didn't want to go to church anymore. He was through with it.

He'd had religion stuffed down his throat all his life, he decided. First by his mother, and then in Sunday school, and then at Hampden Du Bose Academy, where he and his brother Steve had been sent after his father had gone and his mother took over the role of breadwinner.

He'd had religion stuffed down his throat all his life. He reaffirmed this to himself doggedly every time he had a pang of conscience. The church was full of hypocrites, he told himself, the people wore spiritual masks, they were playing church, they were phonies.

He'd gone back finally, but through the back door. The pastor, a lovable and friendly guy, had come to see them and had asked him to play golf. And then he'd asked him to a men's breakfast. Then more golf, and finally, one Sunday morning, Gary announced that he was going along to church.

He and Marianne developed a new set of friends. Two sets of friends, actually; their church friends and their nonchurch friends—two groups whom they hoped fervently would never meet. And he had his own police friends.

His life was neatly compartmentalized, even his temper. You lost your temper at work, but only with your peers, not with the public. You kept your temper with church friends. You could lose it at home, up to the point where you saw the danger signals in Marianne's eyes. You could lose it in front of your mother, but not with her. The idea that you were supposed to control it at all times did not occur to him.

It was a good life, he thought, everything all neatly stacked up and kept in its place. It was a year before he realized he was not happy.

He loved his job, and Marianne still had a figure that

was smashing and still excited him. The children were healthy and bright, and he wasn't in debt—well, not too much. So it was with shock that he stopped in his tracks one day and wondered when the dry rot had set in.

When had the landscaping he'd been so proud of ceased to matter to him and when had his life become dull and when had he known that his mother was less, much less, than a saint and how long had Marianne been a shrew? He felt like something that had been programmed; he was just spewing out what had been fed in.

Then everything tumbled into place, like a kaleidoscope design. It was as if God, who had been so stubbornly slow, had suddenly decided to act.

A group of young people from a huge church in the San Fernando Valley were descending on Simi with a concerted evangelistic campaign. And of all places, they were holding the campaign right in the shopping center.

The first shock came when Gary and Marianne learned that their church would have nothing to do with it, had refused to support it, had forbidden its young people to go over. The second shock came when he and Marianne went over and saw what was going on.

Young people were talking to young people, yes, but to old people, too, from the rich down to the bums. They were praying together, weeping together, laughing together. Something was going on, something they had never seen before, never known before. It was incredible. They went home dazed. And they went back to their church, stunned at the indifference there to the whole phenomena.

The next morning he sat in the choir and looked at the people in the congregation. He *liked* them, he thought. They had been good and kind to him and Marianne; they showed love for one another. But why were they coming to church, warm and friendly and complacent, then going home again and doing nothing outside their own bailiwick? He thought of the song "Little Boxes on the Hillside" that had swept the country a couple of years back, a scathing commentary on housing developments and the establishment, and wondered how they'd react if he stood up and sang a parody:

> Little Christians in churches,
> Little Christians made of ticky-tacky,
> Little Christians in the churches,
> And they all look just the same.
> There's a white one, and a black one,
> And a red one, and a yellow one,
> Little Christians made of ticky-tacky,
> And they all look just the same.

They might not even know the difference, he thought, getting whimsical. They might think it was bona fide, another song like "Red and yellow, black and white, they are precious in His sight, Jesus loves the little children of the world . . . ." He wondered if people really listened to the words of songs, anyhow.

We're like paper dolls you cut out of newspaper and then string out, all exactly alike, he thought. And color one of them me.

After church, they'd eaten their Sunday dinner almost in silence, while the children chattered.

But nothing was ever to be the same again.

The week had gone on as usual, except for Marianne. She'd been on the phone again. Which church, she'd wanted to know, had supported these visiting young people? She'd found out, and they'd gone there to visit the next Sunday.

Even from the parking lot, they had sensed an indefinable spirit of—what was it—love? Yes, but more than that, he thought. It was anticipation. These people were *excited* about going to church.

Where did all these young people come from? They were filing in, with Bibles as big as suitcases, and with such radiant looks he couldn't believe it. Once inside, they were singing softly, reverently, and church had not even started yet; some of them were even raising their arms in an act of worship.

Incredible!

He sat through the service in a daze. He'd never felt this way before. He tried to analyze how he felt. A longing, he supposed, a longing to know God better, to know Him closer, but he couldn't express it. Something was holding him back. All his training was holding him back. You didn't just praise God personally like that. You sat there and read your praise with the congregation out of the weekly bulletin. Still, this was irresistible. They went back. And kept going back.

There was a purity about the worship, an innocence and a vulnerability. It went against all his training, all his preconceptions of what church was supposed to be like. Still, he could not stay away.

The denouement came when the church chartered a bus for a trip to Costa Mesa, to a huge church headed by somebody named Chuck Smith, whoever he was.

Could they go? They went.

After the service, Marianne had given him a sideward glance, a silent plea for understanding, and had gone down the aisle toward the front. He had waited patiently for what seemed to him an interminable time, and then he had gone down to find her. He found her kneeling by a front seat. She had been praying. And when she turned her face up to him, there was a radiance in it that he had never seen before.

They drove home in silence; he was afraid to ask her about it. He went to bed that night resolving to dismiss it all as emotionalism.

In the days that followed, he was both bewildered and angry. In spite of his skepticism, he had to admit that something had happened to Marianne. She was aglow. He was delighted that this had happened to her and bewildered that it had not happened to him. She was a totally different person. Totally his, yes, but a part of her was a mystery to him, new, elusive.

One Sunday night, in a burst of determination, he had gone down the aisle and had knelt before the altar and asked the pastor and elders to pray for him. Whatever it was that Marianne had, he would have it, too. He would *demand* it. He had fooled around with God long enough. It was high time God answered.

As they prayed, he seemed to walk into an immense quiet. He released himself to it and waited. But he got to his feet at last, disappointed. He had felt nothing, not really, not what he had expected. Why was he the same person, and why had he expected something else? And why was all his childhood training still clinging to him?

After that, he awakened in the early mornings to find her up already, out on the patio, and she seemed to be talking to God. She had an insatiable appetite for God's Word; her Bible also seemed to be an extension of herself.

He felt that he was living on the periphery. All this was beyond the pale of his understanding or experience. But he was still living in that quiet he had walked into that night when he had knelt at church. And out of that quiet came the conviction that the denouement was coming, that he was right on the verge of *knowing*.

7

"If Barrett comes out here with Edith, I'll tell you what I'll do. I'm gonna get married right here in the middle of this parking lot, and Barrett is my best man. I'll be married by a priest or a rabbi or a chaplain. All I want is a cop as my best man—" Ken Hermin was saying it all in one breath, but Gary wasn't listening. He was picturing Marianne receiving a posthumous award, with the children standing alongside, and hoping they would be stoic and not cry.

"—and I've got the horn of Gabriel in my lap," Hermin finished. "Sergeant Barrett, are you there?"

"Do you know how to play it?" Gary asked automatically.

"I know how to play it, but I'm damn sure I'm not gonna try to bring the world down, Officer. All I want to do is live in peace."

Gary suddenly wanted to laugh. Why is it that tragedy and danger can be suddenly and unaccountably funny, even for a moment, he thought. Or was he so tired he felt giddy?

"Have you got in touch with his girl or his uncle yet?" Gary asked into the room.

Negative.

"You're starting to sound more like cops, and I'm sure glad, because for a minute I thought someone was going all the way on me," Hermin said.

"No, Ken, your wish is our command," Gary said

55

jovially. Yes, he must be giddy.

"Thank you, sir," said Hermin, and then repeated it ingratiatingly and softly, "Thank you, sir." What made it incongruous was that he meant it.

If this guy ever converted and became a preacher, he could sway millions, Gary thought. In spite of his ramblings, he was immensely articulate, and could play his delivery like an organ, swinging from bass, all stops out, to dulcet and lyrical, all in one sentence.

"This is Captain Judd again," said Judd, breaking in on Gary's thoughts. "When I send Sergeant Barrett out, so that you can identify him properly, he'll be the only one wearing a white helmet. Is that all right?"

I'm a pigeon, Gary thought. A dead one.

"You can understand that my primary interest at this point is your safety and the safety of the other people there who are innocent," Judd went on.

"You've got it. On the line," said Hermin, very businesslike.

"It's very important to me that we have the gun first."

Very important, Gary thought. Make a point of this.

"I'll hand the gun to Edith."

"And it's all right if Barrett accompanies her?"

"He may accompany her if she holds his gun hand. Does he draw right-handed?"

"Yes."

"That's all I want to know. You've got a deal, Officer. Get Barrett and Edith out here, and you've got a deal."

"All right," Judd said, "I want you to keep talking to me while he's out there." He nodded to Gene Smith, indicating that he should drive Gary out.

"You'd better keep talking, man, because I've been wired for a long, long time. This thing is so covered that you'd better listen to me explicitly. The mail slot on the door, remember? If someone sticks anything but Barrett's voice through that mail slot—" And then, off-mike, his voice rising, "Hold it. Hold it!"

"Relax, Ken, relax," Gary said.

"Hold it. I've got a lot of power left, Buster."

"Who are you hollering at, Ken?"

"I'm hollering at my soul, Officer. It is hurting me. It is starting to hurt."

"I'm glad to hear you're trying to control yourself, Ken. That's good."

"I'm trying to do it, Buster."

"That's good, Ken."

"Okay. There it is. I'm back. Are you with me?"

Gary picked up a memo that had been scribbled hurriedly and pushed at him by an officer who had come in from the hall. "We have a problem, Ken," he interrupted. "We have Edith on the phone, and we found out that she lives in West Los Angeles."

"You can get her here."

"It's going to take some time. We're going to send a car over, red light and siren, and pick her up and bring her back. But it's going to take a while. We want to make sure that Chris is going to be okay."

"Hang on a second. I'll guarantee you her life, Officer." And then, off-mike, "Chris, what do you think of me as a person?" There was more talk they could not distinguish. Then Hermin's voice came back. "Chris just said I'm a wonderful person. I swear to God that's what she told me." Then, "Chris, I want you to walk over. I want you to put one hand on top of your head. I've seen this done in the movies. Stand up, Chris. Stand up real slow." He came back to the phone. "She will tell you I'm a wonderful person. She will verify my existence."

"Listen," said Gary, "I believe in your existence—"

Hermin suddenly turned nasty again. "I don't want to get cute. That was a cute remark, Buster, and I don't like it."

"Okay."

"All right, then, let's cut it out."

"We'd like to talk to Chris," Gary said, hoping to get him back on the track.

"Okay," Hermin said, and then spoke to Chris. "I'm gonna tell you how you're gonna do it, Chris. Stand up real slow. Do it right now. I've still got you covered." He spoke into the phone. "I'm going into a bit of action right now, Officer."

"Ease it down," said Gary.

"Okay, I'm gonna ease it down. After she—after she picks up the phone—" He spoke to Chris, "Only by the cord, the dangling cord."

"Yes?" came the other voice.

"Chris? That you?" said Gary. "Are you okay?"

"Yeah, I'm okay. You just do what he wants, okay?"

"Yes," Hermin's voice came in, "tell him I'm for real, Chris."

"Yes, he's for real," Chris's voice came back. "I . . . I really think he's a good person. I don't think any charges should be held against him, whatever happens."

This was a strange phenomenon, the inexplicable affinity of hostage to captive, of the tormented to the tormentor, of the hunted to the hunter. Was it because they were mysteriously bound together in a death lock, Gary wondered, or was it a form of shock?

"Good, we're glad to hear that," he said automatically. And then somebody shoved another memo under his nose. "Listen," he said into the phone, "I'm just being told that Edith is being brought over now, by a West Los Angeles police car, Code Three."

A Street Cop Who Cared

"What's the number on it?" Canny and suspicious.

"I don't know," Gary said, "but I'm sure they haven't tricked you."

"All right," Hermin shot back. "You can get *my* license number in a hurry, so you get the number of that police car."

"Get the number of the police car," Gary said to the room, wearily. "And have you got Uncle Charles yet?"

"He's flown out of town," was the answer.

"Listen," Gary said, taking a new tack, "you're familiar with our ID cards?"

"Yeah. You throw one in the mail slot, and I'll look at it. I'm not bending over to get it. I have a chair, I'm not very far from the door."

"All right, listen," Gary said. Oh, God, make him forget Uncle Charley. "My photograph is on the card, and my serial number. You'll know what I look like before you even see me."

"That's a deal, Buster."

"I'm leaving now, Ken," Gary said. "I'm coming up now." He nodded to Gene Smith, who got up and started for the door.

"You're not wearing a stick and you're not wearing cuffs."

"I'll take the cuffs out."

"What about the stick?"

"I won't wear one."

"Wait'll you see what I look like, man; wait'll you see what I look like."

"I think we'll look like brothers, Ken. I've got some information for you on that police car that's coming from West LA with Edith."

"Let's go," Hermin said.

"The number on it is eight-A-thirty-six. The shop

number will be written on the door of the car. That will be eight-twenty-thirteen.''
"Where is that at?"
"It's on the door of the car."
"Where?"
Gary hesitated for a second.
"It's on the door," he said, "right under the words To Protect and to Serve."

8

Captain Judd had recognized, from the moment he had stepped into the room an hour before, that Sergeant Barrett had already established a rapport with both Ken Hermin and the hostage, so he had kept in the background.

But now Gary Barrett was leaving, and Judd took over. He swung into it with ease, knowing when to talk, what to ask, and when to listen.

Gary left on wooden legs, like a man going to the gallows. Actually, he was so stiff from sitting so long that it was hard to get in motion again. He lumbered through the room, down the hall, and to the outside door, where Officer Smith was waiting to drive him.

Once outside, he was both relieved to get out of the building and repelled by the smog and the promise of heat, already gathering in the early morning. He glanced up at the elevated parking structure, at the housetops, tree tops, and mountains beyond, and he thought of the people out there sleeping or just starting the day, oblivious to the life-and-death drama that was becoming routine to him. Los Angeles was just waking up. He was ready for bed, had been officially off duty hours before. His muscles ached. He wanted to stretch, to run around the block, but there was no time. He went to his car, and before he opened the door, he saw again the sign To Protect and to Serve. "And perchance to die," he thought. Yeah, they ought to add that.

He remembered how, in the beginning, he had told Marianne he was going out to crush crime, but right now he was bone weary, and it all looked pretty silly and futile. It had been months since Marianne's experience at Chuck Smith's church, and months since he had longed for it, and he had felt no dramatic change. He just stayed in that deep quiet, totally alone.

And now he was on his way to confront a maniac who was wired up and had a gun he was banging on the desk, and a hostage.

Gary got into his car and waited while Smith adjusted the mirror and checked his lights, and they pulled out into almost empty streets, Code Three.

He thought of his mother.

"My son is a Los Angeles police officer," she would say, and it was like scraping a fingernail up a blackboard when she said it, as if she'd rather have said, "My son is a minister," or "My son is a missionary." It grated, and underneath, he always fancied he heard a counterpoint of disappointment.

Well, he had become a cop. He liked people. He liked being out on the streets. He liked the excitement, the personal contact. This was life, where it was at.

He *liked* being a cop.

How many suspects emerge as *people*, he wondered. Or for that matter, how many cops? He had never supposed that every cop was necessarily the "good guy." Or every minister or rabbi or priest, or even missionary, for that matter.

He remembered Corrie ten Boom's story about their pastor in Holland, who would not get involved in helping the Jews during Hitler's rampage. "What kind of a Christian was he?" she had asked her father. And he had shaken his head wisely. "Corrie," he'd said, "because a mouse gets into the cookie jar, it doesn't make him a cookie."

Gary checked his map. They weren't too far from the place. He picked up the microphone and switched the police radio over to TAC-two and said, "Nine-L-ten Adam to nine-L-ten on TAC-two."

"Nine-L-ten to nine-L-ten Adam, go ahead."

"Nine-L-ten Adam, inform commander nine that I am about one minute from the location."

"Nine-L-ten Adam, commander nine acknowledges," the voice crackled back.

Gary hung up the microphone and Smith drove on. They were both silent.

He thought of Marianne again. He remembered how she had looked that night at Chuck Smith's church, kneeling by a seat way down front, and the glow that was around her and in her face. He was afraid he'd lost her.

It came full-blown into his mind. Yes, that was it. He was afraid he'd lost her. If he could not follow her into this experience, a part of her would be gone to him forever. He was her husband, but was still first of all the jealous lover. Marianne was his life.

Suddenly, Gary found himself talking to God in his mind. "God, I haven't been much of a Christian, but I want to be. If You'll see me through this and get me out of it in one piece, I'll give You my life. No, wait a minute, God. I'm bargaining with You. I didn't mean to bargain with You. I'm beginning to sound like Hermin."

His prayer stuck in his throat. He *did* sound like Hermin. There was a strange and subtle parallel between Hermin's relationship with him and his relationship with God.

Hermin, stashed away behind his locked door, banging his gun on the desk, shooting into a file cabinet, strutting and demanding. If they brought his uncle—if they brought his girl friend—if Gary would come in with his hands on top of his head like a German prisoner of war—if he could have it all his way—*maybe* he'd surrender. But don't hold your breath. This clown, who had wearied him and frustrated him and stymied his every effort to make peace, this *turkey*.

And Gary, he, himself, stashed away behind his own private locked doors, wielding his own philosophical ammunition, strutting and demanding. Yes, he'd surrender—if God would meet his terms. He had asked Christ to come into his life when he was a boy, and he'd meant it. But for years now, too many years, he had been calling all the shots.

The parallel between Hermin and himself, and himself and God, was almost comical in its absurdity. There was only one difference.

God had never called him a turkey.

"Lord," he blurted out at last in his mind, "I don't mean if You'll see me through this, I'll give my life to You. I mean I'll give my life to You right now, no matter how this comes out. Whether or not I ever 'feel' anything or have an 'experience.' I'm throwing out no conditions. Not anymore. I capitulate completely, on Your terms, God. No arguments." He realized his eyes were stinging.

Smith pulled into the short block that led to the complex. Gary could see several police cars. "All I ask is that You give me wisdom to know what to do and to keep my cool, that's all I ask, God," he thought as Smith pulled up in the only space left, and they both got out.

9

It was an industrial complex, with flat-roofed buildings of various heights and fire escapes cascading down the sides from roof to roof and then to the ground. It abounded with large industrial trash bins.

There were cops all over the place; behind some of the bins, behind police cars, and on the various roofs, all with a bead on that rear door. If a shooting war starts, anything near that door will be pulverized, Gary thought. His thought was immediately verified by several officers standing nearby.

"Barrett, you're crazy to go up there."

"Yeah, you're nuts."

"You're a sitting duck. Are you going to go up?"

He walked around to the driver's side of the car. "I don't have much choice now," he said. He got in and pulled up to a spot about twenty feet from the door.

Another unit pulled in just then, and someone said, "It's the car with his girl friend." He got out of his car and walked over to where she was. She was huddled in the front seat, very frightened.

"Edith, I'm Sergeant Barrett," he said easily, forgetting her last name for a moment and hoping he sounded calm and reassuring. "Have you known Ken long?"

"No, Officer," she said. "Only a few weeks."

"Well, it was awfully good of you to come down. And we won't endanger you in any way. You just stay here in the car, if you will, and we won't call on you for anything, unless we need you. Okay?"

"Okay, Officer," she said. He thanked her and went back to his own car and turned on the P.A. system.

"Ken, can you hear me?" he said. "It's Gary Barrett."

First there was screaming inside. "Hey! You shut up right now." Then the voice came closer, right out of the mail slot, "Barrett, I want you to shut that bullhorn up, you hear me? Shut up right now, 'cause my voice can outlast your bullhorn. You hear me?"

Gary edged his way toward the door, keeping to the side.

"I'm here, Ken," he said.

"I want you to come in with your hands on your head. On your helmet. When I see you, I will release the hammer on the gun, on this three-fifty-seven magnum pistol, Smith and Wesson. It has already proven itself. It can fire. There's a hole in the filing cabinet here that would have put down a bull moose. Can you hear me, Barrett?"

"I hear you, Ken."

"Dump your ID in. I want to look at it. And it better land face up. I can drill this little gal right through the eyes."

Gary fished for his ID card, slipped it carefully through the mail slot, praying it would land face up.

"I've got it," Ken's voice came back. "I've got the card, Barrett. I'm gonna pick it up. I want to tell you, man, I've learned a lot from the movies. I've learned a lot from the CIA movies and the James Bond movies. I've learned it all, and I think then some."

There was a slight pause. "I'm looking at an LAPD card. I'm not too wild about cops. Tell me your mother's name, Barrett. Is that on your card anywhere?"

"No," Gary said, "it isn't."

"I thought you might have your mother's maiden

name on your card. They have that at the bank. Okay, Barrett, tell me your mother's maiden name. Spell it for me."

Spell it? Gary couldn't even remember it—hadn't thought about it for years. But from somewhere, out it came.

"Mac Namee," he said. "It's Scotch. You pronounce the 'ee,' " he added irrelevantly.

"Spell it. Spell it backwards. Quick, Barrett!"

It was highly unlikely that he could spell it forward, Gary thought, but amazingly he did spell it backward, as if he'd been doing it all his life.

"What's your serial number?" Ken shot out next.

Gary gave it.

"Backwards."

Gary recited it automatically, like a schoolboy.

"Say it again—frontwards and backwards—again, forwards, backwards. Okay, Barrett, you checked out. Now count to ten in Spanish."

This was ridiculous, Gary thought. His legs were getting cramped from crouching. He didn't know any Spanish beyond *numero uno*. But even while he was thinking it, he found himself counting in Spanish rapidly, forward and backward. He was speaking in tongues, he thought. It wasn't the way he'd wanted to, it was just the way it turned out.

"Okay, Barrett, here's what's happening. I want to come out. I want to come out into the sunshine. I'm tired of being in this smelly place. I have but one weapon in my hand and here's the deal, here—is—the—deal. I'm standing no more than twelve feet from my target, and I'm deadly accurate . . . ."

"Ken, you wanted me to pray with you, do you remember?" Gary said desperately. Stop him, Lord, he thought. Stop him. Let me get his gun before he comes out.

"Wait a minute. Shut up and let me finish!" the voice screamed. "This is coming to an end and my voice is getting tired and I've been doing too much talkin' for too long and I'm sick and tired of it—"

"Ken, listen to me. You asked me to pray with you—"

"Will you shut up, Barrett? Now shut up and listen to me. I'll tell you how to walk in. I want you to come in with your hands on your helmet. I've got the gun cocked right now. This is the moment of truth, like they say in bullfights—"

He cut off short, and Gary waited, straining toward the door to hear. Hermin was talking, apparently to Judd on the phone.

"I'm making a deal with you right now," he was saying. "You want the hammer down?"

There was a pause. "You've got the hammer down. But I know how to cock this thing in a second."

I've lost him, Gary thought. I've lost contact with him.

"I am holding my trigger finger about two inches away from the trigger guard," Hermin went on. "I'm going all the way. I'm going all the way. Wait a minute."

The pause was excruciating.

"Hey, Barrett, you know what? You told me we were going to pray together, remember?"

The relief was almost unbearable. Gary shifted his weight to the other leg.

"Let's do it," Hermin said. There was a sound of movement on the other side of the door. "I'm kneeling right now. I'm kneeling right now, Barrett. Come by the door and kneel with me."

Was it a trick? "Will you let me take your hand while we kneel?" Gary asked. "Can you get your fingers through the mail slot? I'm kneeling on the other side."

"Okay," the voice came back through the mail slot. "Will you say it with me right now? Will you start it out? The one about the Shepherd." Hermin's fingers came through the mail slot, and Gary grasped them in his own. At that moment, Ken Hermin emerged as a person.

"The Lord is my Shepherd," Gary plunged in, not sure he'd remember all of it. It was easier to say in church than under stress. "I shall not want. He leadeth me beside the still waters . . . ."

"No, I'm talking about . . . . Is that the Lord's Prayer? Oh yeah . . . . I was thinking about the Twenty-third Psalm."

". . . He maketh me to lie down in green pastures," Gary went on.

"Wait a minute. Wait a minute, now. It *is* the Lord's Prayer I mean. I'll say the Lord's Prayer right now with you, Barrett, if you'll start it out."

There was silence in the parking lot. Every man was at his post, gun cocked, waiting. The whole scene had taken on an air of unreality.

"Our Father, who art in heaven," Gary began.

"Our Father, who art in heaven," the voice came back, incredibly. It wasn't a trick.

"Hallowed be thy name." Gary went on, "Thy kingdom come. Thy will be done in earth . . . ."

Hermin jumped in, "Hallowed be thy name. Thy kingdom come. Thy will be done, in art—. No, wait a minute. On earth—I'm—wait a minute, wait a minute, I blew it, man, hold it—"

Silence.

"Take two," Hermin said. "I said 'in art.' Take two."

Nobody's going to believe this, Gary thought.

"Take it from the top," Hermin said matter-of-factly.

"That's a little engineer slang. Let's start it from the top, then. All right. Our Father, who art in heaven—"

"Hallowed be thy name—" Gary went on, Hermin following.

"Hallowed be thy name. Thy kingdom come. Thy will be done—hold it, now. Slow down, Barrett."

The whole thing was tragicomic, Gary thought. This was unreal.

"—In earth, as it is in heaven." Hermin was plunging on. "Is that right?"

"Perfect," Gary said. "I never heard it better."

"Give us this day our daily bread," Hermin said.

"And forgive—" Gary prompted.

There was a pause, then they finished it together, Hermin a word behind. "And forgive us our trespasses, as we forgive our trespassers. And lead us not into temptation, but deliver us from evil: For thine is the kingdom, and the power, and the glory, for ever."

"Amen," Gary finished.

"Amen," came out through the slot after a pause. "I've been to different Sunday schools in my lifetime."

"Then you know that God loves you," Gary said. "And that Jesus Christ died for you—that He is God."

They grasped each other's fingers for a moment longer, then Hermin pulled his away, back through the mail slot.

"The bullets are coming out the mail slot," he said. "Here they come." He dropped them out, one at a time, into Gary's cupped hand. One fell on the pavement and spun and rolled, and Gary got it with his other hand. He counted them. If Hermin was telling the truth, they were all there.

"Can the gun come through?"

"Take my hand, Officer Barrett," the voice came

through the slot again, and the fingers. Gary took them, held them tightly, then let go.

"I'm comin'. I'll come out."

Gary heard the movement as Hermin got to his feet, then the sound of a door being kicked open. The officers inside the building had entered the room.

For a few seconds, Gary couldn't straighten up. Officers were jumping down from fire escapes, and out from behind trash bins, and climbing down from roofs.

"I'm glad you guys didn't have to shoot," he said, straightening up painfully. "It would have been pretty hard to miss me." He shrugged off the backslapping, suddenly embarrassed.

The officers inside were having trouble getting the outside door open, the one with the mail slot.

Gary went around to the front entrance and down a hallway. He passed the place where Hays had been phoning when the shot was fired, and went into an office.

There were several cops in there, one supporting the girl, who was sobbing quietly, two standing on either side of Hermin, at the far end of the room.

"Take her in another office, and get her some coffee," Gary said, and to her, "Do you think you can answer some questions?" He was surprised at how quiet his voice was. He put his arm around the girl's shoulder and gave her a pat, and the officers drew her away.

He stood there then, looking at Hermin, who stared back at him with an expressionless face, suddenly a stranger. The bushy beard and long, dark hair somehow did not go with the voice.

The voice had been vibrant. There had been an inexplicable winsomeness about the man, but this gangly, sweat-soaked apparition, with the vapid face and empty eyes, was a total stranger. Gary felt exhaustion, then rage, as he stood and stared. This mindless monster, he thought, who, by waving a gun, could keep an assortment of at least twenty cops dancing attendance and asking how high every time he said jump.

The rage left him as quickly as it had come. He walked up to Hermin and stood holding his gaze for a few seconds, then lifted his arms slowly and put his hands on either side of Hermin's face.

This gesture surprised him. He hadn't intended to do it. He hadn't even thought about doing it. He looked intently into Hermin's eyes, as if by looking, he could demand some sign, some signal, some clue that would help him understand. But the eyes that looked back at him were empty, as if Hermin had closed a door and any communication between them was finished. Hermin was living a long way behind his eyes, way off somewhere where nobody could touch him.

"Ken?" Gary said.

There was no answer. The room was very quiet, the only sounds were voices off in another part of the building and outside in the parking lot. After a few seconds, Gary dropped his hands, and two officers steered Hermin toward the door. "Take him easy," Gary said.

He turned to the phone someone was holding out to him.

"This is Barrett. Is anyone there?" he said.

"Yeah. This is Judd, Barrett."

"You owe me a steak."

They both laughed with relief. "What are you doing for lunch?" Judd said.

"I can't stick around that long."

"Then let's go to breakfast right now. And you can have your steak."

"Okay."

"We'll see you back here."

"See you soon—" Gary began, but Judd had hung up.

He was astonished to see it come out in the news the following day, but more astonished to see the headlines in the various papers:

"Musician Holds Hostage, Sings Hymns With Police"

"Officer's Hymns End Siege With Gunman"

"Policeman Pleads, Prays, Holds Hand of Gunman in Drama at Sound Studio"

"Twenty-four Hours of Terror in Studio, Hymns End Gun Play, Barricade"

And, in each paper, the copy ran along the same line:

"Barrett went up to the front door and began talking to Hermin. In attempts to get Hermin to turn over his gun, the officer linked hands with the suspect through the mail slot in the door and recited the Lord's Prayer . . . ."

"Barrett, talking through the locked door, established a rapport with Hermin, who had the sergeant sing hymns and recite the Lord's Prayer and the 23rd Psalm . . . ."

"Singing hymns and reciting prayers, a police sergeant today calmed and captured a distraught rock musician . . . ."

"A Van Nuys police sergeant pleaded, prayed and through a mail slot in a door, held the hand of a trumpet player for a tense two hours before the man, who had threatened to shoot a hostage . . . ."

"The sergeant had not come alone, but the other policemen were powerless to help until the gun could be talked away from the musician . . . ."

" 'Thy will be done' was recited with more emotion than usual by a deranged musician and the policeman who had come voluntarily to help him . . . ."

It was enough to be hated and branded as pig; to be discredited by judges and manipulating attorneys; to give a justifiable citation expecting anything from verbal abuse to a bullet in the gut; to be used by parents to frighten children; to spend one-third of his twenty-four allotted hours being hated, or at best, tolerated.

Now he would be known among his colleagues as "that Christian turkey."

Judd's report was lengthy, several pages, and in considerable detail. And it had the same emphasis:

> Barrett engaged deft. in conversation to occupy deft's attention . . . . They conversed about numerous subjects and entered the area of religion. Sergeant Barrett and the deft. talked several minutes on the topic of religion, deft. becoming periodically enraged and screaming obscenities and threatening the life of the hostage. Sergeant Barrett would again bring up the topic of religion and the deft. would calm down . . . .

Gary winced as he read it; what a ribbing he would take for this! And it got worse.

> Sergeant Barrett, disregarding all personal safety, moved to a position beside the front door, completely exposing himself . . . . Sergeant Barrett engaged in another religious conversation and the deft. wanted to shake his hand. Deft. opened the mail slot in the door with his hand and Sergeant Barrett, in turn, again completely exposing his person to the deft's line of fire, moved in front of the door and grasped the deft's fingers. Deft. seemed to calm down greatly. Sergeant Barrett maintained his exposed position. At this time

deft. informed officers that he was unarmed and threw his remaining bullets out the mail slot to Sergeant Barrett . . . .

I broke every rule in the book, Gary thought. When the dust settles, I'm going to get a lacing from Judd and a ribbing from every cop in the division.

But instead, they gave him the Medal of Valor.

10

The lights in the Hollywood Palladium were blinding.

Gary stood backstage, waiting his turn. He tried to think of the dignity of the moment, but his mind, perversely, went on a tangential spree.

He thought of the hassle in getting the family ready that morning, how Marianne had finally cried out, "Why didn't you ask them to *mail* you the medal?" The absurdity of quarreling on such a morning had struck them both, and they had fallen back on the bed, laughing.

As each recipient was called onstage, Gary found himself thinking, "Ten little, nine little, eight little Indians, seven little, six little, five little Indians, four little—"

And then the producer signaled for him.

And cool and crisp on the outside, and sweating on the inside, Gary went through his paces. Twelve steps up to the platform, as he had been coached. Jack Webb's voice boomed out all over the Palladium.

Jack Webb, he thought, his thing, the voice he grew up with, his hero, doing the narration. It was shattering. He was really primed by the time he hit the top step.

And then all his peripheral vision went. He had only tunnel vision, seeing just Chief Davis, and the chief seemed such a long way away. It was the longest walk Gary ever took in his life. The applause seemed to drown him as he took it. Then Chief Davis draped the medal around his neck and saluted, and Gary remembered to salute very properly and to make a right about-face and go up on the risers and stand there in his spot till the remaining few got their awards.

Here I stand in all my splendor, he thought. And suddenly he wanted to laugh. He remembered his kid brother Steve being in a play back in school, maybe in the fourth grade, and wearing a magnificent toreador costume. "I don't have to do much," he'd explained to the family at home. "I just stand there in all my splendor."

After a while, Gary's muscles began to ache as he stood at attention on the riser, trying to remember whether Webb's narration had had a Christian emphasis.

When he finally remembered that Webb had said, "Sergeant Barrett prayed with the suspect," his booming voice filling the huge cavernous room, Gary did not have time to react, for the program was suddenly over, and his mind split into fragments.

Somewhere up on the top tier, his mother was gathering up his children. His eyes sought out the spot where his table had been. Marianne would be sitting there, waiting for him. It was hard to spot, for people had risen and were milling around, backslapping and crowding the open spaces; except for the few who headed for the bar, nobody seemed in a hurry to leave. He strained his eyes to see who was still sitting, and when he spotted Marianne, his mind ground to a halt. She was calmly gathering up the leftover rolls from their table.

The stage was jammed with well-wishers, relatives, backslappers, reporters, and cameramen who had rushed up the steps or vaulted the huge stage apron.

Moments later, Marianne was beside him, and then the children were turned loose by his mother and they came up, suddenly shy and strange in the glare of the camera lights. They were placed together as a family, then nudged along, as though on an assembly line, to be interviewed for radio and TV and to have their pictures taken with the notables.

He answered questions easily, faintly surprised that he was articulate after the tension. Marianne's voice was quaky, on a higher pitch than usual. Suddenly he realized she was terrified. She had a quick wit in private conversations, but before the awesome reporters, she was like a frightened schoolgirl.

It was rather fun to see her thrown like that. He found himself torn between amusement and guilt for enjoying her discomfiture, and decided on amusement. Get yourself out of this one, gabby, he thought in wicked glee, as she struggled in vain to control her voice and her trembling hands.

Then their pictures, with Marty Milner, with Jack "Just-the-facts-ma'am" Webb, the big man himself. Jack shook hands with them, and Gary could not wipe the grin off his face.

There was an air of camaraderie about it, almost of naiveté, if you did not pick up the somber contrapuntal theme underneath—see, we are only pretending for today that it is all glamour and glory. Tomorrow we'll go back to riding the streets and walking the back alleys alone, knowing that at any turn we could find a beaten child or a raped and mutilated girl, or confront a madman who will hurl abuse at us for upholding the very laws that enable him to be there, or stop a bullet.

Then they were out in the parking lot, all talking at once, Marianne with her bag of rolls tucked under her arm. She was beaming, his mother's eyes were spilling over, and he hated to end it. But more cars were backing out, and he came back to earth with a thud. He had to go to work at five the next morning, and home was a long way away.

"I'm taking the kids with me," his mother said. "I'm parked out on the street."

They all walked to her car and tucked her and the children in. She rolled the window down and gave him a look of such love and pride that he was embarrassed and hoped she would not say anything just then. She could be loquacious on occasion, time was getting short, and she'd better get the show on the road before one of the kids had to go to the bathroom. To his relief, she pulled out into the traffic almost at once, the children thumped on the windows, calling good-byes, and they were gone.

He turned back to Marianne. They both grinned, and headed back to their car.

"And now the coach turns into a pumpkin," Gary said as he pulled into the traffic out on the street. "Let's take the slow way home."

"Mother's taking the kids for tonight," she said, "so there's no hurry. Turn left up here."

He did.

"Left again," she said. He did, and they were on Hollywood Boulevard, going west. "Just keep driving," she said. And finally, "Now left in there." They were in the Hollywood Roosevelt Hotel parking lot.

He pulled the car to a stop, "Now what?"

"We have a reservation," she said triumphantly. "Wait here, and I'll check it out." She scrambled out of the car. "Our luggage is in the back," she called over her shoulder.

He could do nothing but grin after her as she hurried in through the rear entrance of the hotel. Bless her. This meant that he would be much closer to work tomorrow morning. But more importantly, they'd have more time together. He was still grinning as she emerged, until she got closer to the car and he saw the look of consternation on her face.

Before he had a chance to ask, she answered. "They

won't take my check," she said incredulously, "I have ID, but they won't accept it." Her disappointment was so great that he felt sorrier for her than he did for himself. Her surprise was spoiled, and it was an inestimable loss.

"Hold it," he said, managing a faint grin as he fished in his pockets. He handed her his ID and his badge. "Here's all of it, the works," he said. "I'll go park and meet you inside." She took it and turned to go. "And don't worry," he said, "they'll take the check. If I have to haul in the Medal of Valor."

She was at the desk when he got inside, writing a check. "They'll take a check, but only for the price of the room," she said. He nodded, and went back for the luggage. Hotel policy was sacrosanct; he felt an argument would be useless and degrading for him. He did not have a cent in his pockets to back it up. He hoped Marianne had the price of a meal.

She did not.

Up in their room, he looked at her incredulously. "No money at all?" he said. She looked stricken. Her surprise was slowly coming apart—now it was nearly in shambles.

She recovered before he did. "The rolls," she said, and without a word they both went toward the door. In the elevator they were not alone, so there was no chance to talk. They walked to the car in silence, too, and without a word started stuffing rolls in their clothing. When they got back to their room they unloaded them all on the dresser. She pulled the last one from her waistband.

They both laughed then, and she dived back into her purse and rummaged through it, feeling the bottom, like someone rummaging through a drawer for a lost sock, and finally held her hands triumphantly aloft.

"Three dollars!" she cried, "Three dollars!" She

dumped the contents of the purse on the dresser. "And almost a dollar in change!"

She was ecstatic. "We can take a walk later and get something to go with the rolls," she said, and dived for the suitcase and opened it. "Some cheese and something to drink and maybe even some butter." She hauled out the clothing she had packed and threw it on a chair, and then flung herself on the bed, laughing.

"I haven't walked down Hollywood Boulevard hand in hand with you in a long time," he said, and sat on the edge of the bed. They were silent for a minute, remembering. "I keep expecting to hear the intercom," he said finally. "I keep expecting to hear the children's voices."

"Today the children are your mother's joy," she said as she made room for him on the bed. "And you are mine."

That evening they walked up and down Hollywood Boulevard hand in hand, looking in shop windows and mingling with the crowds. The shops dealing in magic and witchcraft were legion, the streets were awash with weird costumes and shaved heads and cultists passing out sticks of punk.

"It wasn't the same," she said later.

He turned on his side and looked at the luminous clock. It was 2:30 A.M. "What wasn't?" he said.

"Hollywood Boulevard," she said. "It wasn't the same."

"What do you mean?"

"We're not kids anymore."

He was silent for a moment. "I know what you mean."

They lay there in the quiet for a few minutes. The light filtered in through the window, casting a ghostly glow over their strewn clothes and disheveled room. He was suddenly awake.

"D'you know?" he said, "I think I know now what's behind the corny speeches they make at the Academy Awards."

She waited.

He struggled for words. "I mean, the way they thank everybody."

She didn't answer. He thought she might have fallen asleep again, but he went on, as if to himself. "Take the guy who held up the sign inside the studio. Johnson. I didn't know it at the time, but he printed in crayon on a big piece of paper, 'Don't do anything until we tell you to.'

"But then he had to get the hostage to read it without attracting Hermin's attention. So he kept slipping out from behind the window jam so the hostage could see him holding the sign. He had to keep his eye on Hermin at the same time. Hermin was wired up and jumpy and so *quick* that Johnson exposed himself to getting shot I don't know how many times before the hostage nodded that she understood.

"And the rest of those cops. Their restraint. They could have rushed him, probably, and got the hostage shot, but the whole idea was to see that nobody got killed or hurt. I was crouched outside, I didn't think about it then, but there was as much tension and drama inside as out, I suppose.

"And Sergeant Hays. He was on the other side of that wall, in a phone booth. When Hermin fired that shot, he fired it into a file cabinet at the exact spot where Hays was phoning on the other side of the wall. If it hadn't been for a phone book in the cabinet, the bullet could have gone through the wall and hit Hays. The bullet landed in the phone book. Mine wasn't the only life in danger. And Captain Judd, talking to Hermin, keeping him occupied until I got there."

He went on, completely awake now and warming to his subject. It seemed important to relive it. He was like an author reliving his play after he'd come away from opening night, going over the good spots and the places where things had gone wrong and trying to figure out how they could be improved. He knew he would not be able to sleep at all, but the prospect of a sleepless night did not worry him. He figured he had enough adrenaline in him to carry him through the next day.

But then the phone rang.

"Good morning, Mr. Barrett, it's four A.M."

Somewhere in the midst of his ponderous and lengthy discourse, he had fallen asleep after all. Marianne was sleeping like a child, her breathing barely audible. He leaned over and kissed her softly, then got out of bed and headed for the shower.

Now the coach would turn into a pumpkin. She would drop him off at work and then go on home. And the Medal of Valor award would, within months, probably be forgotten.

11

It was ninety in Simi Valley, with a forecast of a hundred and ten. Gary started to embrace Marianne when he left for work, thought better of it, kissed her gingerly on the forehead instead, and tasted salt. When he got into his car, his shirt was already wet and sticking to his back.

The freeway was just as bad. He was blasted with hot air coming in from the open windows, and the exhaust from other cars burned his nostrils.

The Palladium and the Medal of Valor seemed far away. The backslapping and the congratulations were like things he might have fantasied. "What d'you know," he had said to Marianne within weeks after it all happened, "I'm just a bum again."

Ken Hermin seemed even farther away. Gary had gone to the Van Nuys jail to see him the day after his arrest, but talking to him had been impossible; he had still been so strung out he had made no more sense than he had made back in the studio.

But later, at the hearing, Gary had found him to be a different person, well-spoken, his beard and hair clipped, his manner subdued and contrite. The hostage had refused to testify, and the case had been dismissed after a series of hearings.

Now it all seemed far away and unimportant.

Gary got off the freeway at last, and drove slowly through the broiling streets. Now there was not even hot air blowing, just still and stagnant heat and smog.

Inside the station it was several degrees cooler. He went to the locker room, showered, and got into his uniform. He started for the roll-call room, then realized he was twenty minutes early. John Kingsley was standing outside the door, leaning against the wall, a cup of coffee in his hand. Gary bought some from the machine and went over and stood alongside him.

John was an affable guy, tall and medium built, with a shock of blond hair. "Barrett!" he said, grinning. "You too? I can't think of a lousier day to be out in the field."

"I know," Gary said, taking a cautious sip of the hot coffee. "I wish I were home, soaking in a cold tub."

"I wish I were out at my beach house," John said. "But I haven't got a day off for a week."

"You have a beach house?" Gary asked, incredulous. A beach house sounded like heaven.

"Well, it isn't much, just a small one. I hope to move out there someday and fix it up and live there. Right now I just rent it out when I'm not using it. But only to cops."

There were officers piling in the roll-call room now, so Gary and John went on in, found seats together, and sat down. There was an assortment of officers in there—street cops and sergeants, some young, some old-timers.

"Did you see Archer?" one of them said.

"Who, Frank Archer?" this from one of the old-timers.

The first one nodded.

"No. Why? Is he coming on or going off?"

"He's going off. He stopped for some coffee. He's white around the gills. I didn't think he was going to make it to the locker room."

"Why?"

"They called for a unit with a camera, and he had the

department camera with him, so he answered the call. Went to Bel Air."

"What was it?"

"Suicide. The guy was sprawled in the bathroom, his head behind the toilet. Shot himself in the head. I guess he was a bloody mess."

There was a little silence.

"Did the guy leave a note?" somebody said.

"Yeah," said the old-timer. "Something about the fact that he'd achieved everything there was to achieve. Even the street he lived on was named after him."

"Then what was wrong?"

"He wrote that without love at home, he'd achieved nothing. I don't know who didn't love him. I suppose his wife left him, or something."

Gary thought of Marianne back home, her face drawn and weary, tendrils of curly hair damp on her cheeks. He turned suddenly to John. "Is there anybody in your beach house now?" he said.

"No, it's empty. Want it?"

"Could I have it?"

"Sure," John said. He took a bunch of keys out of his pocket and put them on the table in front of Gary.

The desk officer came in then, and Lieutenant Cowper, who started droning out the names for roll call before he'd hardly settled in his chair.

As soon as roll call was over and the assignments made, Gary headed for a pay phone.

"Listen," he said when Marianne answered. "Don't talk. Just get a sitter. And get packed for the beach. Because when I get home, that's where we're going. Just the two of us."

There was a silence, and then a shriek of delight.

A couple of hours later, they were headed north on the

freeway, the hot air blasting their faces, the traffic blasting their eardrums. "It's a total assault on all your senses," Marianne shouted.

"What?"

"It's a total assault," she shouted more shrilly, "—never mind!"

They drove the rest of the way in silence, until he turned off the freeway and headed west, toward the beach.

"Feel the cool," he said a few minutes later, as they neared a beach community that looked as if it belonged somewhere in Europe and should be open only to bicycles; it seemed almost an offense to drive a car there. The streets were narrow asphalt lanes, lined with drifting sand and houses of every size and description, and every vintage. They ranged from small to large to very large— and from funky to luxurious.

John's house was a small, neat bungalow, nestled comfortably in the midst of high oleander bushes and flaming bougainvillea.

But they looked at it without seeing. Without a word, they kicked off their shoes, got out of the car, and headed for the beach. As soon as their bare feet felt the sand, they started running. Gary slowed down as they neared the water, preparing to stop, until he realized Marianne had no idea of stopping. She kept running toward the wave that was coming. The water broke over her ankles, but she kept going until it hit her knees and slowed her pace. Then she ploughed ahead with giant steps, lifting her leg high with each step, until she was floundering, hip deep. She kept going, and he followed her until they were up to their necks. The next wave swept over their heads, and they came up shrieking, Marianne's hair streaming in her face.

They ate dinner at a place filled with an assortment of tables and chairs, no two alike, and a sandy floor. They ate fish and clams greedily, licking their fingers, and sat in contented silence afterward, looking at the vast expanse of sea, silver gray, hurling itself at the beach only a few feet away from where they were sitting.

By the time they got back to the house and made the bed, they were so exhausted they crawled in and were both asleep almost immediately. The surf pounded, but they never heard it.

The next morning, Gary awakened to the sound of the sea gulls' weird cries. He felt for Marianne, and then smelled the coffee. She was already up.

Moments later, they were drinking coffee on the small balcony, where they watched the ocean through and around an assortment of chimneys. "I'd like to go for a long walk," Marianne said. "A long and aimless walk, leading nowhere, the way we used to when we were dating."

He smiled, remembering. Most of their dates would wind up on the beach, and most of the walks would wind up with cheesecake and coffee at El's in Westwood Village. "Maybe we can find some cheesecake and coffee," he said aloud. "The way we used to."

"Can we eat breakfast out?" she asked. "Do you mind?"

"As long as I can wear shorts and sneakers and my T-shirt with the arms cut out, I don't mind anything," he said.

"We'll do better than that," she said. "Let's go barefoot."

Afterward, he thought it was a perfect day, more perfect even than the elysian days of their honeymoon on San Francisco Bay.

They walked and lay in the sand and talked and drowsed and waded in the water when it got too hot and walked again.

"We've had everything but the cheesecake," Marianne said as they were walking back.

Gary let go of her hand abruptly and made a dive for a stray volleyball that had come out of nowhere. He threw it toward a blond fellow who was holding his hands out for it. There were about a dozen people playing volleyball. The blond fellow caught it expertly. "Come on, play!" he shouted.

Without a word, Marianne darted forward, Gary on her heels. They each took a different side, and Gary hoped he'd remember the rules. They came back almost at once, along with his touch and coordination.

Marianne shrieked in dismay when she missed and shrieked with delight when she didn't, and he felt an exhilaration and a delight in her that he had not felt in months. Why didn't this side of people show up when the children were quarreling underfoot and the washing machine broke and the gophers got into the grass and the temperature was 110?

After the game, they were invited to go along for supper at a house a few hundred yards down the beach. They went along like children—it never occurred to them not to. They helped with the barbecued fish and the salad. And afterward, they all trooped in the house and sat on the floor and stairs when the chairs gave out.

Some of them sang, swaying from side to side with the rhythm, ballads, and surprisingly innocent songs.

Gary overheard a dark, bespectacled young man ask Marianne what the fish meant that she was wearing about her neck. "Are you a Pisces?" he asked her.

"No, this is an Ichthus," she told him. "That's the

Greek word for fish. See, the Greek letter for *I* is the first letter in the word Jesus. And the Greek letter for *CH*, or *X*, is the first letter in Christ. And *TH* is the first letter in God. *U* is the first letter in Son, and *S*, the first letter in Saviour. So you've got *Jesus Christ—God's Son—Saviour*. See?"

She said it with candor and with a childlike freedom and, yes, with joy, he thought. He had always thought witnessing was a serious and ponderous business. He had never been able to do it without a constriction in his throat and a slight rise in blood pressure.

But she was telling this guy about Jesus as if she were offering him a treasure, the key to life itself, and it suddenly struck him that she was.

Then they played games. "Can you believe it?" Marianne said softly to him out of the side of her mouth. "I used to play some of these in high school."

"If you were going to be on a desert island all alone, what would you bring?" someone was saying, and Marianne looked at Gary knowingly, as if to say, "See what I mean?"

The answers started coming out, around the circle, and she stopped looking at Gary long enough to give her answer when her turn came.

"A Bible," she said promptly, and the lad she had explained the fish to, said, "I figured you'd say that."

Then the games began to peter out, and Gary pressed against Marianne with his shoulder to get her attention.

"I think we'd better go now," he said. He stood up without waiting for an answer and helped her to her feet.

Marianne said nothing as they walked slowly back to the house. "We had to leave," he said, answering her unspoken question. "I had a feeling it was about time for them to break out the pot. I just didn't want to be there to see it. Just for these few days, I don't want to be a cop."

She slid her arm around his waist and they went on, trying to match steps and failing, then broke into a run and raced for the house.

On the last day, they lolled on the beach in the morning, then decided to drive around and get acquainted with the whole area in the afternoon. They drove along leisurely, stopping to let dogs and children cross the road, and even pulled up to one house with a FOR SALE sign on it and got out to snoop.

They crouched under some untamed branches that had jutted out over the walk from two unpruned myoporum trees, and tried the front door.

It was a funny little house; square, with a second story built on the back half of it like an afterthought, for the stairway to it was on the outside. They peered through the windows, which were all ceiling to floor and took up two sides of an L-shaped living room, flanking a fireplace.

They walked around to the sides and back and peered through smaller windows into the bedrooms. Then they scrambled back into the van, looking back at the upstairs windows and balcony as they drove slowly away.

A mile or so up the road they passed a realtor's office and pulled up and went in to inquire about the house, the way young girls try on clothes in stores with no intention of buying. The realtor spotted them at once for "no-buys," told them the price, and went back to her books with a nod that was definitely a dismissal.

They started to leave, but at the door Gary made her an offer, an absurdly low one, and she said, "Be serious, now." But she was smiling, and they left in a spirit of merriment.

Late that afternoon, they drank in one last sunset.

Then, reluctantly, they packed up the car and headed for home.

Simi Valley was still hot, but not as hot as before. The respite had done them good. Even their own bed felt good, Gary thought. He felt refreshed and revived, and incredibly happy. He settled alongside Marianne with a long, loud sigh and they lay there in silence that was heavy with unspoken words.

"You know, that house drew me," Marianne said at last. "It *drew* me."

"It drew me, too," he said. "But I think we're both beach happy. The house is part of the whole picture."

She did not answer. Not long after that, she was breathing evenly, sleeping like a child.

We've got a house twice as good as that monstrosity, for half the price, he thought as he drifted off himself.

"Don't shoot, Mr. Hermin. Please don't shoot," Sergeant Gary Barrett begs the hostage-holding gunman Ken Hermin, whose call to Los Angeles police station demanded Barrett's quick, levelheaded thinking.

Hermin's threat, "You're gonna save a girl's life by bringing the lady I love," launches a city-wide search to bring Hermin's girl friend, Edith, to the besieged recording studio.

"Lord, I don't mean if You'll see me through this, I'll give my life to You. I mean, I'll give my life to You right now, no matter how this comes out," Barrett prays before confronting Hermin.

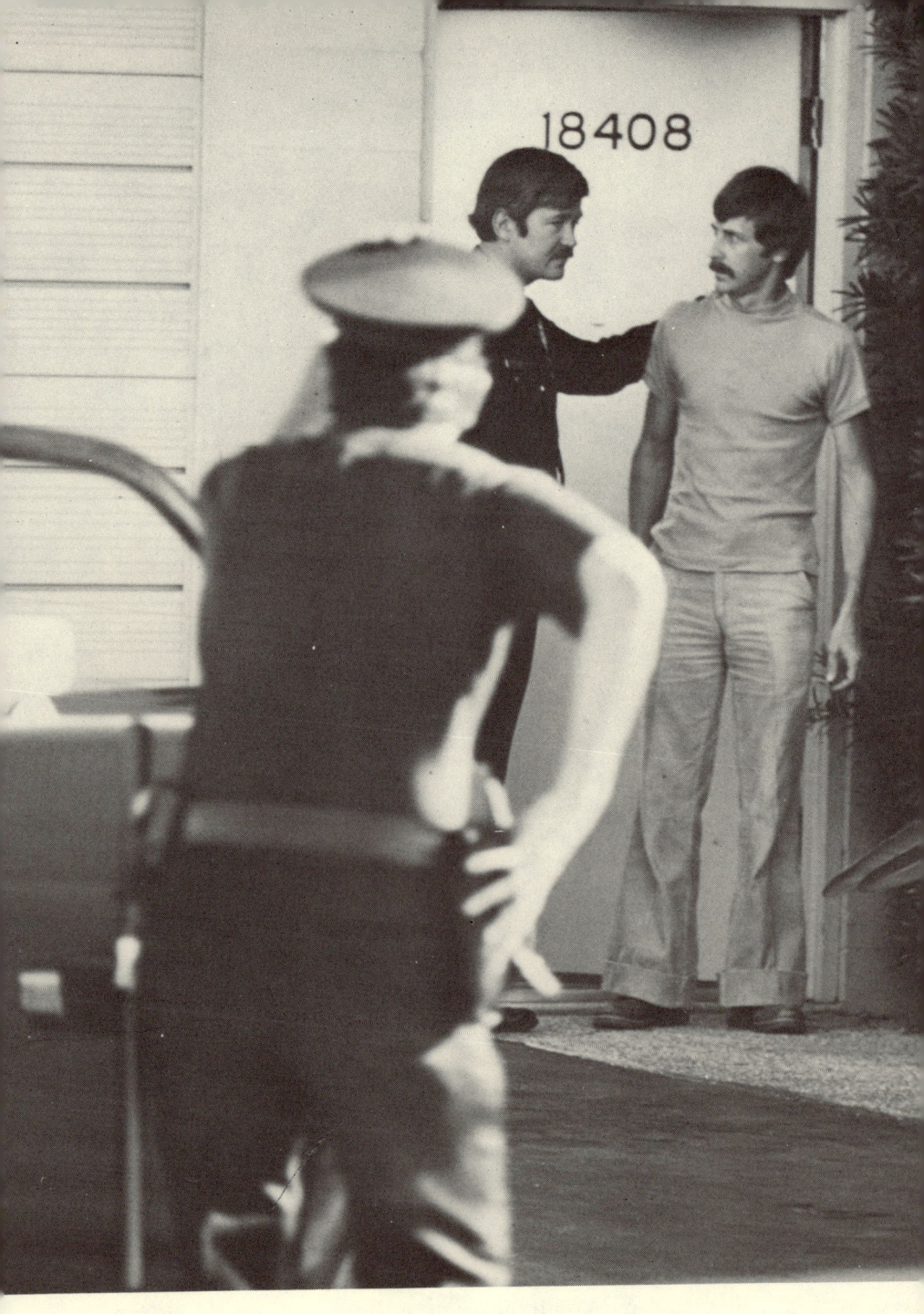

After haltingly praying the Lord's Prayer through the door with Barrett, Hermin gives up the gun, his hostage, and himself—and the voice emerges as a person.

Chris, the hostage whose fate was held by the whim of the deranged Hermin, is freed through Barrett's courage—for which he was awarded the Medal of Valor.

"I just have the conviction that God wants us here at the beach—*this* beach," Gary tells Marianne—the beginning of their ministry.

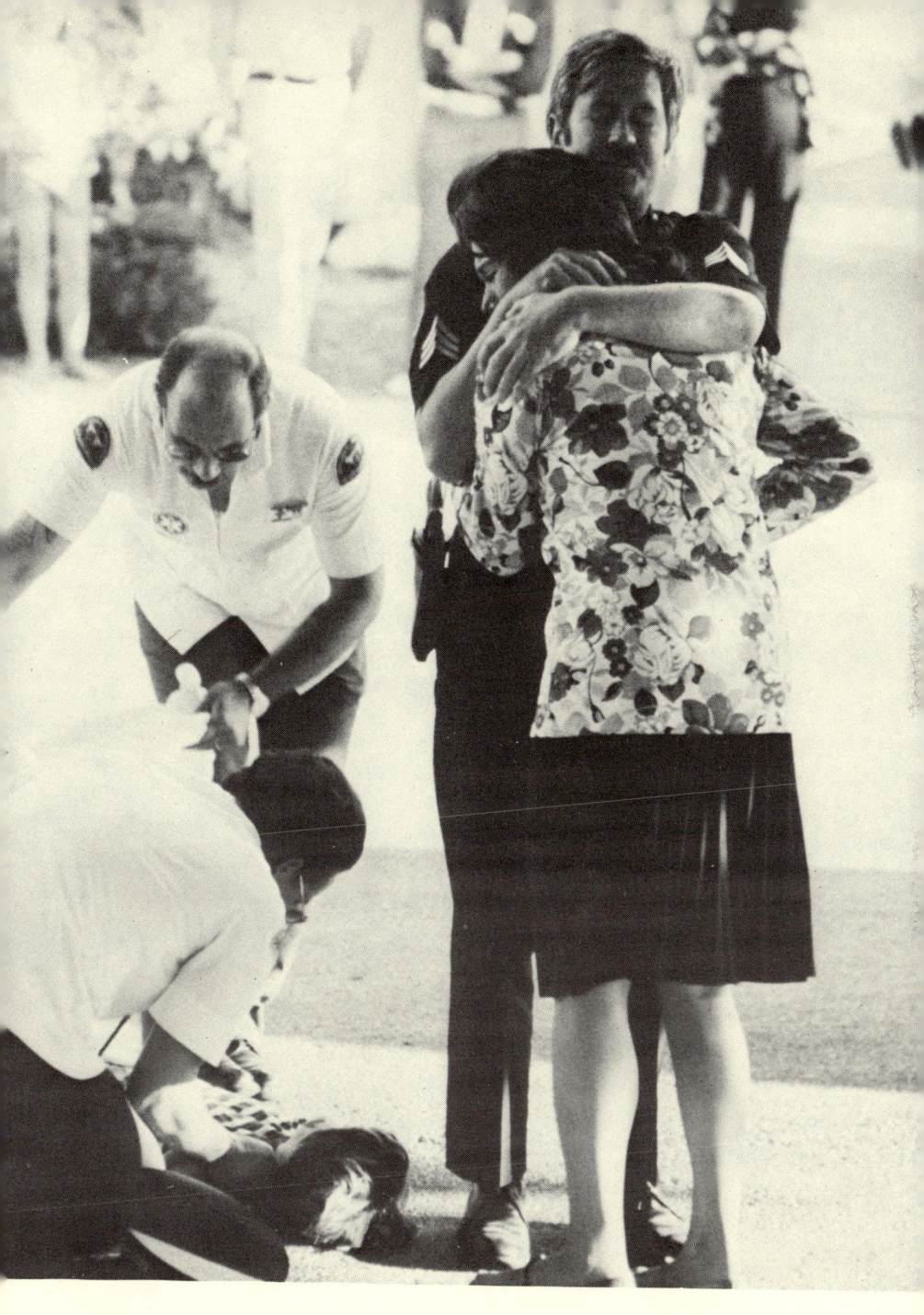

Weeping with those who weep, as Jesus did, Barrett shares the agony of a mother whose child was just killed by a car.

The production crew makes last-minute lighting and sound adjustments on the set of a stakeout scene from Outreach Films' motion picture *BARRETT*.

12

"The day is young. Let's go to the beach," Gary said suddenly, as if he had just thought of it, though he knew he'd been thinking about it with one part of his mind for days.

It had been a week since he and Marianne had been out there, and he had not been able to get the beach house off his mind.

"Would you like to go to the beach?" he asked again. The kids were ecstatic; Marianne said nothing, just looked at him and began stacking the dishwasher.

Twenty-five minutes later, they turned off the freeway and headed west. He did not go to John's beach house, though, as she knew he would not. He drove across the channel and pulled up in front of the square, ugly house with the FOR SALE sign in front, and stopped.

The children piled out first and headed for the beach. "Wait a minute," he said. "First I want you to look at this house." They followed him, ducking under the recalcitrant myoporum branches, and began peering into the windows.

"It's great," they said. "Is it haunted?"

It must look worse than he thought. Haunted?

"No," he said. "Would you like to live here?"

Their answer came in a chorus of shrieks. As they headed for the beach, he stood there with Marianne, who was still peering through a front window, squinting, trying to see down the hall to the bedrooms beyond.

103

"Do you still feel that this house is drawing you?" he asked quietly.

"Yes." But it was said with a solemn calm, not excited at all. "I do. I really do."

Without a word, they headed for the beach, toward the children. They dug places in the sand and sat there quietly, watching the surf and the sailboats beyond.

"Are we going to buy it, Dad?" Mike asked.

"I don't know," he said. "But if God wants us to have this house, He'll let us buy it. I think we should talk to Him about it. Right now."

They gathered in a tight little circle, and for a long moment there was silence, with only the cry of the sea gulls and the pounding of the surf.

"God, it sure would be neat if we could have this house," Mike said at last.

"God, if You want us to have this house, we'd sure be willing," from Sean.

"Dear Jesus," Michelle said, "it would be great if we could have this house. Even if it looks crummy and like it didn't have too many bathrooms."

Then he and Marianne prayed, following their simple pattern, even using the word *neat*.

After the children had left to go shell hunting, they both sat there silent, watching the late sailboats come in.

"Do you think we're crazy?" she said at last.

"If we are," he said, "God will check us."

He dug his toes in the sand. "I just have this conviction," he said at last, "that God wants us here on the beach. *This* beach. Right back there in that house."

Later, back at the realtor's office, his confidence ebbed a bit. "I'm making the same offer," he said, before they got halfway through the door, "and I'm—"

"No," she smiled.

"—serious," he finished lamely. "We've even prayed about it."

Though she was still smiling, she had the closed face of a banker or an accountant. She thought in dollars and cents, not in the nebulous world of dreams and feelings, and certainly not in prayer.

"Could you let us know the name of the owner? I'd at least like him to hear our offer, to talk to him."

"You know I can't do that." Her smile was patient. "The doctor put it in my hands because he does not want to be bothered with buyers. He's in the middle of a divorce."

They thanked her and left. "Well, at least we know the owner is a doctor," Marianne said. "That's more than we knew before. Maybe we can wear the realtor down."

"Third from the left, second row," Marianne whispered, nodding toward the choir Sunday morning.

"What about her?" Gary said.

"Vera Arnold," she said. "She's a realtor."

He reached over and squeezed her hand. At that moment the choir burst out with Carmichael's "Something Good Is Going to Happen to You," and he squeezed her hand again.

Vera was doubtful when they talked to her after church. "Ordinarily we don't traffic in other realtors' territory," she said. "But if she refused to take your offer to the seller, then I think it would probably be okay for me to—" She hesitated a moment. "I can check the county records and find out who the seller is for you. I can do that much. I'll give you a ring sometime tomorrow."

She did better than that. "Quick," she said when she phoned, "I have an appointment with the owner. Tell me, what are we offering?"

When Gary told her, there was an imperceptible pause, then a low whistle. "No wonder the realtor at the beach wasn't impressed," she said. "But I'll give it a try. Will you go any higher if the doctor says no?"

"I'm afraid not," Gary said. "That's as high as we can go."

After he hung up, they stared at each other for a full minute in silence. Then, "We'd better pray," Marianne said at last. "Right now."

When Vera phoned back the next day, it was obvious that they had better pray.

"Do you think you can sell your present house in two weeks?" she said.

"Two *weeks?*" Gary said, incredulous.

"Well, that's the length of time the owner will take the house off the market and hold it for you."

"Are you saying what I think you're saying?" he said.

"Yup," Vera said. "The doctor has accepted your offer."

Gary shifted his weight to the other foot and back again. Then he realized he was cracking his knuckles. He cracked his knuckles—or so he had been told—when he was either very tense or very bored. Right now he wasn't conscious of being either—only of the fact that time was dragging.

The week had been interminable, without one nibble on the house, and without one incident to justify the To Protect and to Serve that was printed on his car.

Right now he was having an amiable chat with a bookstore proprietor over a sidewalk display that was

A Street Cop Who Cared

blocking pedestrian traffic. They had already come to terms on the fact that the display should be pulled in closer to the store, and had launched into a discussion on which books were moving, and which were not, and why.

But part of Gary's mind had splintered off and was focused on something across the street. There was a girl standing against a building, and two young chaps, inconspicuous in the anonymity of jeans and T-shirts, facing her, their hands braced against the building. Okay so far, he thought, but the girl seemed to be crying. Maybe he'd get a chance to go out and crush crime after all.

He excused himself and started toward the curb, but the two chaps moved on, walking slowly, and the girl started to cross the street to his side. When she got close, he saw that she was blinded by tears, fishing for a handkerchief. He stepped out in front of her and she stopped, startled.

"Are you okay?" he said.

"I guess so." She had found the handkerchief and was dabbing at her eyes.

"Were those guys bothering you?" he said, looking past her across the street. They were still there, walking slowly. They could still be had.

"No," she said, "they were trying to help me, too. They were trying to tell me about Jesus."

Jesus? he thought, I can't believe it.

"And they were praying with me," she said, as if she couldn't believe it, either.

"Well, that's great," he said. "And what did you think about it. How did that grab you?"

She looked at him in astonishment. "I'm *Jewish*," she said.

He restrained a grin. "So what else is new?" he said

solemnly. "And you didn't answer my question. What do you think of Jesus?"

She hesitated, but only for a moment. "I think He's a heavy dude in history, but He is not my Messiah," she said.

He nodded solemnly. "Would it blow your mind," he asked, "if I said that they were telling you the truth?"

She looked at him in total disbelief.

"And," he went on, "that I'm going to tell you the exact same thing? That Jesus can help you with your problem?" He watched the struggle in her face; it was almost comical to see her try to rally her forces.

"I know," he said. "First you get it from two strange guys, and then a cop stops you and tells you the same thing. Are you a practicing Jew? I mean, do you mean it—your religion?"

"No," she said, glad to get off on another tack. "I'm a nothing. I don't believe anything. And I missed my bus; I gotta go."

"Where are you going?"

"Off Wilshire. It's about twenty blocks down."

"Right on my way," he said. "I made you miss your bus, so I'll take you there."

She climbed into the front of his car, both relieved and embarrassed. He talked to her about Jesus all the way to her corner. This time she was silent.

"There's a Gospel church two blocks on down," he said as he dropped her off.

"What's a Gospel church?"

"Good News," he said. "Maybe you'd better check it out."

"Thanks. I really mean that. Thanks," she said.

He pulled away, checked his watch, and headed back

to the station. His interminable shift was over, and tomorrow was his day off.

When he got home, Marianne came running out to meet him. "We're going to own a piece of the beach!" she shouted.

The house in Simi had been sold.

13

Within a few weeks of moving to the beach, Marianne was living several roles, and to the hilt. She plunged into the business of being a new member of the community with gusto, baking bread and rolls and carrying them in baskets to neighbors.

The role of the policeman's wife she knew all too painfully well. The moment it became known, you were looked at askance, as if you had married some kind of monster, or at best, a latent sadist who could not possibly get along in any other profession.

Gary knew it well, too; the sudden look of withdrawal, the guarded tones, the inevitable launching into long and complaining diatribes of unfair tickets and mean, always mean, cops. They had both learned the art of evasion and how to change the subject deftly with a smile. If all else failed, Gary fell back on his boyhood hero's comment in a Dragnet show: "Yes, ma'am, but police departments still recruit from the human race," saying it with variations, until he began, after a while, to think it was his own.

The role of Christians they lived on several levels. They pasted their silver Ichthus in the window, and the Jesus sticker. Marianne handed out Jesus papers on the beach, and recruited all the children who wandered through the house to do the same.

Her other level was not altogether to his liking. She wanted to work in the deli part-time, after school started.

"There are stacks of underground papers and the *Harbor News* on the deli counter, and I can stack our Jesus papers right next to them. I have a button. I bought it in the Christian bookstore." She produced it, a huge white button with Guess Who's Coming? printed on it. "When customers ask me," she said matter-of-factly, "I'll just tell them Jesus is."

The level that showed the least and produced the most was their secret talks, far into the night, and their prayers. He marveled that they could pray together so naturally and easily now. They had never been able to before. But now he felt a new sense of purpose, a sense of being in that place at that time for a definite reason.

"But what's the reason?" he kept saying at the end of all their talks.

"Well, at least," she would say, "by now they all know we're Jesus freaks. And we're praying. Something's *got* to happen."

He had scribbled part of his thoughts on a card that had a view of the ocean on it, and mailed it to her soon after they'd moved.

> Stacy,
> We are truly rich. Let's not lose our perspective. I praise God for His outpouring of mercy in our lives and for you especially. I feel that we really do know each other better and in a new and exciting way. I somehow feel that some new adventures are just around the corner for us and I can't think of anyone more adventuresome or exciting to do them with.
> Me

Mike had seen the card lying on the desk. "Why does Dad call you Stacy?" he asked after he'd read it.

Marianne grinned back at him. "That's a closely guarded secret," she'd said, and all his coaxing could not make her say any more.

"Four-fifteen, see the family dispute."

It was 3 A.M. when Gary got the call. He grinned at his partner. "It's a four-fifteen," he said. "Right up your alley." His partner was Mike Crenshaw, a pastor from the Seal Beach area. But that night he was a police chaplain. The LAPD had started a police chaplain's corps; the idea was to assign them to different areas, and their job was to help settle family disputes, or counsel, or talk people out of suicide. In general, they were to add a touch of expertise and of the spiritual in tense situations.

The place turned out to be in the Wilshire district, in an apartment neighborhood. The streets were lined with parked cars, as the streets always were in those neighborhoods, but Gary parked as close as he could. As soon as he turned off the motor, they could hear the reason for the call. A woman was having a fight with someone, a ten-decible fight.

They didn't stop to check the mailbox, but headed for the elevator. Gary pressed the top-floor button, and they went up. When they got off, the screams were deafening. They turned right, following the sound, and stopped at the apartment from which it was coming.

Gary knocked on the door, and the screaming stopped suddenly. Then the door opened, and a man stood there—young—probably around thirty. Without a word, he opened the door wide, stepped back, and let them in. There were two officers in the room, one leaning against a desk, scribbling in a notebook, the other sitting on a davenport beside a teenage girl. There was a woman in her late twenties standing in the kitchen doorway, obviously intending to stay out of it.

"Brother and sister," the officer with the notebook said, indicating the man who had opened the door and the girl on the davenport.

"I came home tonight with my friend," the man said, glancing at the woman in the doorway. "And this kid's giving a party. A bunch of kids. My apartment full of kids."

"And can't I have a party?" the girl on the davenport shrieked. "I take care of the apartment, and I get your meals—"

She lunged forward and made a dive for a broken ashtray on the coffee table. The officer pushed it out of her reach.

"She tried to commit suicide," her brother started to explain. "She tried to cut her wrists."

"Nobody cares about me!" she yelled.

"I care about you!" her brother shouted and started toward her. "Hell, don't I take care of you? Don't I?" She lurched at him, striking wildly in the air.

Mike went over to the man, touched him lightly on the elbow, motioned him and the woman out to the kitchen.

"We care about you," Gary began.

"Nobody cares about me!" she shrieked again.

"Where do you go to school?" he said, trying another tack.

"University High," she spat at him, her voice only slightly lowered. "And I work as a box girl in a market, too. I'm earning my own money to buy my own car."

Mike came back in the room then, went over to the girl, and sat down Indian style on the floor in front of her.

"Will you listen to me for a minute?" he said. She looked at him suspiciously.

Gary got up from the davenport, motioning to the other officers to follow him into the kitchen. They stood around, leaning against the counters; Gary positioned himself so he could see Mike and the girl.

"What do you do?" he said to the brother.

"I'm a flight instructor. She jumps on me when I don't go along with her schedule, as if she were my mother or my wife. She's only my kid sister. And she had no right to have a party here. Bunch of kids. A whole bunch of kids in my apartment."

"What were they doing?" Gary said. "Boozing?"

"No."

"Smoking pot? Disturbing the peace?"

"No."

"She sounds like a pretty good kid to me," Gary said. "She's holding down a high-school schedule, a job in a market, earning money to buy her own car, cleaning your apartment, and getting your dinner. I'd say she can't have much time to get in trouble."

The screaming had stopped in the next room. They could hear only low voices.

"What are they doing?" the brother said. "Why can't we go in?"

"You're not going to believe this," Gary said, "but they're praying."

"*Praying?*"

Gary nodded.

In a few minutes, Mike came out in the kitchen. "This little gal has no one to talk to," he said softly to the brother, "especially a woman. She's just jumped from adolescence to adulthood. She's trying to be an adult, and she's never had time to be a kid." Then he abruptly changed the subject. "Did she take her mother's death hard?"

The brother hesitated, then, "I don't think so," he said. "No more than you'd expect. She didn't carry on too much. In fact, she was very quiet about it."

"She feels very guilty about it," Mike said.

"She never told me how she felt."

"You never asked her how she felt."

The brother was silent.

"All her frustrations, everything she's been holding inside, just came gushing out all at once," Mike went on, "when you humiliated her in front of her friends."

"What did you say to her that made her quiet down?" the brother asked.

"I introduced her to the one Person who had the answer to her problem," Mike said. "I told her that when she has no one to talk to, Jesus is here, and she can always talk to Him. I told her that He cares about her, that He is God, who died for her, and that He wants her to invite Him into her life, into her heart."

"And?" The brother's face was a question.

"And she did," Mike said quietly.

The brother started toward the door, and Mike stepped by to let him pass. He went into the living room and the rest followed. The girl was sitting quietly. She was dabbing at her eyes and blowing her nose, otherwise, completely composed. It was a miracle.

Gary and Mike left then. Mike turned in the doorway and grinned at the girl. She managed a faint smile back.

"Don't forget what I told you," Mike said. "I'll keep in touch."

"Okay," she said. "Thanks."

"That was beautiful," Gary said in the elevator. "That was totally beautiful. It was hard to believe what I was seeing. Did you leave her something? A tract?"

"I left her a tract," Mike said, "but that's not enough. I can put her in touch with a church, so she'll have some Christian friends and a social life."

Out in the car, Gary threw a small paper booklet on Mike's lap. "I'm writing a tract," he said. "A policemen's tract."

"No kidding? What made you think of that?"

"Well, I took a young girl to the airport," Gary said, "and I put her on a plane for home. She was a runaway, got sucked into prostitution, and was a virtual prisoner in Bel Air. She managed to sneak a phone call to her mother back in the Midwest, and that's how we came in.

"Anyhow, on the way to the airport, I tried to get an opening to talk to her about Jesus. I tried a couple, three times, I guess, but every time I got started, the cop who was riding with me jumped in and got the conversation off on another tack. I was so frustrated I went home and sketched out that thing."

Mike turned on the map light. " 'Who cares?' " he read. " 'Who cares that you're alone and afraid—that you feel like a loser—' Hey, this is great. And your police car and cop artwork is terrific."

"I didn't draw those," Gary said. "I just rough sketched what I wanted and wrote the copy and chose the Scripture. Lori Siqueido—she's a gal we know on the beach, a Christian, and an excellent artist—she took my sketches and really jazzed them up. She managed to draw a tough cop who also looked compassionate."

They both chuckled.

"Well, the idea is," Gary said, "this is a Christian cop,

and he *cares*, and he has something great to tell you. It's a quick way to do it. You aren't witnessing on LAPD's time. You can just drop it in a purse or stick it in a pocket and ask them to read it."

"You've got a ministry, Gary," Mike said.

"Oh—yeah. And I appreciate it. But the Lord seems to keep telling me I've got one out on the beach, too. There's only one problem."

"What's that?"

"He hasn't told me what it is yet."

14

Gary went down to his locker, took off his uniform, and changed to slacks and sweatshirt and tennis shoes. It had been a sullen and smoggy day. He was glad to be going home.

Although they'd been out on the beach for only a year, it seemed to Gary that they had never lived anywhere else. It held an endless fascination for him. The beach and sea and sky combined to dole out their treasures in infinite variety. There were no two days precisely alike.

They had two dogs now, ginger Dobermans, shiny and graceful, and more affectionate than he had ever realized Dobes could be.

Marianne was handing out her Jesus papers with good-natured abandon, and answering the inevitable questions about her "Guess Who's Coming?" button. She was bringing home accounts of her conversations with customers, too, and slowly the names began to emerge as people.

But we're not really getting anywhere, he thought. Nobody, not one person, has become a Christian because of us.

The closest they had come to Christian fellowship in their home was when Steve and Nancy Robbins, from the Simi Valley church, had brought their young people up for a weekend retreat. Steve was the youth pastor there.

He was medium height, muscular, with dark, styled hair and moustache, and a white-toothed grin. He looked the intellectual behind his mod glasses and spoke in a rapid staccato. His brilliance would have been intimidating, except for a sharp and disarming wit; he could be outrageously funny.

Nancy was delicately pretty, with an aura of fragility about her, a Dresden china quality.

Then Steve and Nancy had begun to come out by themselves, just to rest and get away. "Come on out for a couple of days," Marianne would say. "The sea is healing."

"It draws me," Steve would say each time. "This beach *draws* me."

"Those were the very words Marianne used," Gary would answer. "Only it drew us here to stay."

The year had been one round of parties, inviting friends in, and, for Marianne, the deli, and later taking classes at Ventura College three days a week and juggling Little League and PTA.

The laundry came out of the drier faster than it could be folded during these days, and it piled up on the red davenport in the den relentlessly; it became a Sisyphean task to diminish it, so much so, that once when she had managed to clear it all away, Steve Robbins came by and said in mild surprise, "I never knew that sofa was there," and they were never quite sure if he meant it.

To Gary, it seemed like a year wasted. Even two weeks in the mountains with Marianne and the kids had not changed his perspective. He thought about the sense of purpose he'd had, the sense of excitement and anticipation. All he could come up with now was zilch.

He opened the door, fishing for his car keys, and the smog stung his nostrils. He started for his car in the parking lot, when he noticed some officers over at the other end of the lot, four or five of them, standing over someone.

"Sarge? Can you come here for a minute?"

He went over at a trot, slowed down to a walk as he got closer. It was a woman. They were trying to lift her to her feet, but as fast as they got her up, she slid from their grasp and fell down again.

"Get her in the car," he said to the others. "And take her home. Don't book her."

Inside the car, before they closed the door, she said, "I've tried everything, Sergeant. I got kids at home. They're home alone now. I just can't stop."

"The officers are going to take you home," he said. "And they'll get your address. I'll come and see you soon. And here, read this." He handed her the policemen's tract.

He told Marianne about it when he got home.

"How old was she?" she said.

"I'm not sure. I think she was around thirty," he said. "Anyhow, she was a young woman, and she had children at home."

Marianne's face was working. He was coming home with tales like this all the time. He was surprised that this was hitting her so hard. "She lives only a couple of blocks from the station," he said. "I'll go see her."

Marianne's face suddenly came apart. "Can we pray for her, Gary? I think we should."

His legs were clamped around the bar stool, and he was too tired to get up, but he put his elbows on the kitchen counter and began to pray for this woman whose name he didn't even know. When Marianne began to pray, he was again surprised at her intensity; she was really feeling this.

"O God," she said, "please help this woman. I can

understand, because she's the same age as I am and she's got children the same as I have and maybe they're the same age too. God, where is it written that she should get that way and I shouldn't? And she has kids—"

She couldn't finish. She broke down, sobbing. She had her hands resting on the counter. Gary reached over and put a hand on top of one of hers. "I'm going to see her, honey. I'll talk to her."

"Okay," she said finally. She sat there, her elbows on the counter, her head in her hands. It was several minutes before she stirred. "You got some mail today," she said. "It was mailed to the police station while we were gone. They forwarded it." She pushed a square envelope that was lying on the counter toward him.

He opened it. It was a card. He stared at it for a long time, longer than it took to read the one sentence written on it. Then he handed it to her.

She read it quickly, handed it back. "The postmark was so faint I couldn't make it out," she said. "Who do you suppose it's from?"

He had a hunch who it was from, but he shrugged negative. "It's been just a year since you celebrated a birthday through a mail slot," she said.

He read the card again. It said simply, "Thanks for your faith, and for giving me another year of life."

"We found a fish!" Sean came running up to the Dutch door.

"If he's dead, bury him," Gary said. "We can't use a dead fish around here."

"No, it's my summer-school teacher, Mr. Duerner. And he's got a fish like ours. An Ichthus!"

"An *Ichthus?*" Marianne came around from the snack bar. "You're serious?"

"Yes," he insisted. "We even talked with him. Mike and I talked with him. He lives right down the road!"

"I wish somebody got that excited because I lived right down the road," Gary said. "Where's Mike?"

"He's playing with 'Bug-a-Loo.' He's our class parakeet, but Mr. Duerner brought him home for the weekend."

Gary and Marianne looked at each other, both grinning almost comically in unabashed delight. "Can you believe it?" she said. "Can you believe it?" He couldn't answer, couldn't wipe the grin off his face.

"What'll we do?" she said. "Go up there and introduce ourselves?"

"Why not?" he said, still grinning.

"Right now?" Marianne was asking, but she was already halfway out the door. They piled out and started down the narrow walk. On the other side of the myoporum tree, they came face-to-face with Mike.

"Sean says you've met some Christians!" Marianne said, and then stopped. Mike's face was blanched, his eyes both frightened and pleading.

"Yes," he said. "He invited me up to his balcony."

"Well, that's great," Gary said. "So?"

"So I went up, and I was playing with the parakeet."

Nobody dared speak, and the unspoken question hung heavy in the air.

"I stuck my hand in the cage to pet him," Mike's voice trailed off like a treble run in minor, retarding hopelessly.

Gary heard Marianne suck in her breath. "Oh no," she whispered as she let it out.

"He got out." Mike verified their worst fears. "And he flew away." His remorse was so great that anything in the way of berating would have been cruel at that moment. They gave him the gift of silence.

"We still have to go down," Gary said, "and tell him we'll buy another parakeet tomorrow."

They all dragged down the road as if they were going to a wake. We've met our first Christian friends on the beach, Gary mused to himself.

Marianne unwittingly finished his thought. "What a way to meet them," she said.

He couldn't answer. He was too busy making up his speech for the moment when he would come face-to-face with the formidable Mr. Duerner.

The Duerners' beach house was just like the others that surrounded it, respectable and arty, and on the balcony was the empty parakeet cage and the formidable Mr. Duerner. A young man, handsome and tanned, in yellow shorts and T-shirt, looking down, grinning. His wife Cyndy emerged, immaculate in white shorts and T-shirt, her hair in braids, looking like a young Dinah Shore.

They were both school teachers, the Duerners explained, and yes, they were both Christians.

They discussed the business of an amicable settlement, Gary letting Mike sweat through it by himself and offer to buy another parakeet. Mike would, of course, borrow the money from his father and earn the money to pay him back. It was done in a solemn but friendly manner, but Gary was gratified to note that Mike's voice was a bit shaky.

"I hope we see them soon and often," Marianne said after they got home. "We've waited so long. And aren't they great?"

How soon and how great they found out an hour later.

First there was the knock on their Dutch door, then Fred Duerner's face poked through, grinning. "Look," he said, "is Mike still up?"

Mike came around from the bathroom, his face still steamy from his shower.

"Mike," Fred Duerner said, "I forgive you. I forgave you before, but not completely. Now I forgive you completely. You don't have to buy a new parakeet. *I'll* buy a new parakeet, and we'll forget the whole thing. But you must promise me something."

"Yeah?" Mike said, still wary.

"You must promise me that the next time somebody does something to you that you don't like, you'll forgive him. Okay?"

"Okay," Mike said in relief and surprise.

Gary walked Fred out the path to the road, Marianne following. They exchanged the "Let's-get-together's," and then he was gone.

"Can you believe it?" Marianne said.

He looked at Fred, disappearing down the road. "Incredible," he said. "Totally incredible."

15

Gary and Marianne ran into the Duerners sooner than they expected. On Sunday they went to the second service of a church in Ventura, and got there just as the first service was getting out.

"It's my fish teacher," Sean said in awe, as if he had just run into Gabriel. "It's Mr. Duerner, with the Ichthus in his window."

They all worked their way toward the side, where they were out of the traffic, and Gary introduced the Duerners to the young man he and Marianne had brought to church with them. "Our friend Sam," he said. He was amused at their brief looks of surprise. Sam was grimy and definitely subculture, complete with black leather jacket, beard, and black, curly hair escaping from under a black beret.

"Can you come over for coffee this afternoon?" Gary said.

"Can you go sailing first?" Fred said.

"They've got a sailboat?" Sean said, round-eyed.

There was a quick aside from Marianne. "Shh," she said. "Don't be greedy." She turned back to the adults, but not before Gary saw the faint gleam of covetousness in her own eyes.

They named the time quickly. The crowd was pouring into the church now, and latecomers didn't get seats. As they turned to go in, Gary hung back briefly. "Sam won't be coming with us," he explained quickly. "He's just passing through. He's hitchhiking on up the coast today, but we asked him if he'd come to church with us first."

He turned and followed them in, wondering briefly if Sam was going to take off his beret in church. He did not, and Gary found it did not matter, as long as he was there. "Lord," he said, "I don't care about his hat. Just open his ears."

"We've been out here for months—almost a year," Marianne was saying. "We've tried everything, and nothing's happened. Absolutely nothing, until we met you." She was passing out mugs of hot steaming cider with cinnamon sticks. It was four o'clock now, and the day was clear and sunny, but crisp. They were chilly from the sail.

"We tried, too, when we first moved out here," Cyndy began.

"Sam left his hat," Mike said in surprise, "and he's gone."

"I saw him drive by in your old Volkswagen," Fred said. "Isn't he coming back?"

"Nope," Gary said. "We tried to give it to him, but he wouldn't take it as a gift. So I sold it to him for a dollar. Handed him the pink slip, told him to think about what we'd said about Jesus, and sent him on his way."

"You gave it to him for a dollar?" Fred said.

"Sure," said Gary. "It's got two hundred thousand miles on it, and it's a piece of junk. But he's a good mechanic. He'll get another ten thousand out of it."

"We went from house to house knocking on doors," Cyndy picked up her thought again, "but they were slammed in our faces."

"That's the hardest thing to do," Marianne said. "I passed out Jesus papers, and we invited neighbors in. I even baked bread and took it around, but we never knocked on doors. I don't think I have that kind of courage."

"There's no way these people can be enticed into town," Fred said. "They don't want to dress up. They want to stay in their shorts or their bathing suits, so they'll be ready to jump when the surfing waves are just right. It's a different culture."

"There ought to be a church out here," Gary said. "That's the thing that would really work."

"That's been tried," Fred said. "Twice—no, I think three times—churches in town have tried to start mission churches out here. You know, branches, supported by the mother church. They all folded. They never got off the ground."

"Or we could offer our homes for beach parties," Marianne said. "Invite young people from other churches. We could supply the showers and a place to change clothes."

"Yeah, we've already done that," Gary said. "It works. The young people from our old church in Simi Valley have been up here. And the youth pastor and his wife have been here, too, just by themselves, to get away and rest."

The sun had gone down now and the chill was blowing in from the sea. He got up and lighted the fire, and Marianne headed for the kitchen to raid the cupboards, but Fred and Cyndy had to go.

"We've been praying about this for years," Fred said in parting.

"Well, now there are four of us praying," Marianne laughed. "Meet your reinforcements."

"It's got to be more than that," Gary found himself saying. "It's got to be more than just praying."

"It's got to be more than that," he said again, much later. He and Marianne had decided to sleep downstairs by the fireplace, and the only light was from the embers, now glowing. There was no answer. The Dobes lifted their sleepy heads, grunted, and laid them back down again.

"Are you awake?" he whispered.

"We haven't been specific!" she cried, getting up on one elbow so quickly he jumped.

"Let's pray every night this week, *specifically*. And be *urgent* about it," she said, warming to her subject.

"Okay," he said. "I'm game."

"And ask God to give us an answer by next Sunday," she went on quickly, getting bolder.

"Now wait a minute," he said. "I'm no minister. I'm a cop. Don't pray me into something I can't do."

"I'm not praying *you* into anything," she said, "we're praying the beach into having a church, that's all. Let's start, let's do it right now."

They lay there together, holding hands, looking up into the dark of the vaulted beam ceiling. Their prayers were simple but urgent, interrupting each other's.

"If I pour myself out like this every night," he thought afterward, "I'll run out of things to say by Wednesday."

But by Wednesday he was totally involved in the thing, consumed by it. It suddenly seemed the most important thing in life, to get God's mind on the idea by Sunday. He supposed it was because he had never been this bold before.

By Friday he was crying out, "Lord, I'm no minister, and I can't get out there and preach. But I'll do it if I have to."

On Saturday, Steve and Nancy came out. At the first opportunity, Gary thought, I'm going to tell them we've been praying all week. Maybe God's answer will be to have Steve tell us what to do.

He cornered Marianne in the kitchen and told her.

"Of course," she said. "Why else would they just drop in like this on Saturday? God's going to tell us a whole day early."

She waited until the children were out of the house. Then, "Well, tell him, Gary," she said. "Ask him."

Gary opened his mouth with that intention, but instead he said, "You know, you're going to be our beach minister."

"Whaaat!" Steve laughed. "Oh, sure."

"Don't knock it," Gary said, and then found he didn't know where to go from there. Steve had a paying ministry, Nancy was nearly nine months pregnant. The whole thing was ludicrous, why had he said it?

"Don't knock it," he said again, lamely. There was a strange silence, which seemed somehow spiritual rather than actual, for the surf was still pounding outside and the gulls were still crying overhead.

Steve broke it with more laughter, but it simmered down to a soft chuckle and trailed off.

They talked about getting a beach ministry started then, but it was general, and Gary did not mention again the idea he had blurted out at the beginning, until they were leaving.

"Think about it," he said, grinning, indicating that he was aware of how foolish it sounded and that, of course, he hadn't meant it.

But on Sunday he found himself saying to Fred, "I've got a guy who would be great as our minister, if we had a church."

"You mean he'd come?" Fred was incredulous.

"I mean we could always ask him," Gary said, and

waited. They were all walking along the beach, headed home after a sail.

"Where would we get the church?" Gary expected Fred to answer. "And where would we get the money?"

But instead, Fred said, "I've got a house I always felt the Lord had given me. If we really could get something started, we could use that house."

They all walked a few steps in silence, then suddenly broke into a run, as if on signal. Fred and Cyndy made for their house down the road, heading for their car. Gary and Marianne and the children piled into their Datsun and crawled along slowly until they got abreast, then they all went down the road in a sudden fever of excitement. A mile up the beach, Fred stopped in front of a huge, white house enclosed with a high wall and boasting a profusion of foliage. They pulled to a stop behind Fred's car and stared, round-eyed, then they all piled out of the car at once, and stood there, speechless. "I'd let it go for just the mortgage payments," Fred said at last. It came out as if he'd just thought of it—which he had—and as if he was surprised that he said it—which he was.

He turned and started back to the main entrance, which was on the side. All of them followed mutely, like school children on a field trip, and they stood aside with a respectful silence as he unlocked the door.

Their excitement simmered down to awe as they snooped into each room, treading softly, as if they expected it to disappear.

They parted outside, speaking in noncommittal and cautious terms, as if they would perhaps go too far, past the point of no return.

Once back home, Gary and Marianne faced each other, and each of them took a deep breath and let it out slowly.

"Well, we asked the Lord for an answer by Sunday," she said at last. "Are you scared?"

"It isn't that I'm scared. It's just that I don't know where we're headed."

"Well, the Lord has told us to start a church," she insisted. "He just hasn't told us *when*."

"We don't have any money," he said. "Not a cent."

"I know," she said, and her eyes were dancing.

He grinned, and then they laughed, outrageously, with shrieks and guffaws; Gary ran for the harbor, where Mike's Sabot was tied up, Mike running after him. They piled in and paddled furiously toward the breakwater. Once at the breakwater, he turned and saw that Marianne had run out on the beach, Michelle and Sean with her.

He lifted his arms up, threw his head back, and shouted, "Praise the Lord!" He watched as she threw her arms up and, head back, shouted something he could not hear. But he knew it was, "Praise the Lord!" as he watched her standing there, her hair tossed back, her face upraised to the sunset.

16

Gary was southbound on Gayley Avenue in Westwood Village. He passed the theater where *The Exorcist* was playing; he'd passed it many times when the line was a block long, but it was 1 A.M. now, and it was all quiet.

About two blocks past the theater, he saw the figure on the curb. Probably a drunk who had to sit down before he fell down, he thought.

He stopped the car, got out cautiously. He had no back-up, no partner; this was no time to be careless. The man had not moved when Gary had parked. He had apparently not seen him coming.

Gary positioned himself slightly behind him and said very quietly, "Is there anything I can do to help you?"

The man lifted his head slowly and then, just as slowly, looked around. It struck Gary at once that the man was not drunk, nor was he a bum.

He looked at Gary in surprise. "You actually stopped to ask me if there was anything you could do to help?" he said. He shifted his weight until he was facing front again, put his head in his hands, and started to cry.

Gary let him go on for a moment, impatient now. Maybe he'd been wrong, maybe the guy was a drunk after all. "Tell me," he said over the sobbing, "what are you doing here?"

The man lifted his head out of his hands long enough to say, "I've been to see *The Exorcist*." Then he stopped crying, fished out a handkerchief, and blew his nose. A long shudder went through him.

135

Gary waited.

"I've been to see it three times," the man went on. "I didn't want to see it. I wasn't going to see it. But finally I just couldn't *not* see it. Can you understand that?"

Without waiting for an answer, he went on. "I was just *pulled* in there. I was pulled in there, as if by some unknown force. I know what you're thinking, the joke about 'The devil made me do it,' but it's not funny. I really *was* pulled in there by some unknown force, and I can't laugh it off."

"I'm not laughing at you," Gary said. "Go on."

"Well, I ran out the first time, before it was over. I didn't get up and walk out; I ran out as fast as I could run. But I couldn't get it off my mind. Then a few nights later, I went back and saw it again. I saw it through that time. I was nailed to my seat, I couldn't get up. As soon as it was over, I ran out again. And then—" his voice began to tremble again, "darned if I didn't go back and see it a third time. Tonight was the third time. I ran out and I ran up the street and stopped here. I just couldn't seem to move. I've been sitting here. I don't know how long I've been sitting here."

Gary took a step closer, leaned over, put his hand on the man's shoulder. "Don't let that movie psych you out," he said. "God is stronger than any evil force that could possibly psych you out. You've just plugged yourself into the wrong source, the wrong power."

"What do you mean?"

"Plug yourself into the power of God." He fished out a tract and slipped it into the man's breast pocket. "Read this when you get home."

Gary prayed for the man then, a quick prayer, and he couldn't remember afterward one word he'd said. Then he helped him to his feet. "Will you be all right?" Gary said. "Do you want me to call you a cab? I can call it from my car."

"No. I'll be all right," the man said. When he stood up, Gary could see that he was expensively dressed, and now that he could speak more calmly, apparently well-educated. "I have a car," he said, "just a block and a half from here. And I'm better now. I can drive home. I don't live far from here."

The man was still thanking him as Gary got into his car and pulled slowly away from the curb. The guy's mind was sure blown, Gary thought as he turned south on Midvale and started back to the station. He couldn't decide whether he and Marianne should go see *The Exorcist* to find out why, or whether they should stay as far away from it as they could.

Suddenly, he slowed down. He wondered if he had imagined it. He had just passed an alley where he had seen, or thought he had seen, a small flare, as if somebody had lighted a match. It was down close to the ground, as if somebody was sitting down. He decided not to back up. He turned right at the next corner, right again, and cut around to the other end of the alley. He drove slowly into it, past long rows of carports on either side, and pulled up and stopped his car.

He'd been right. There was somebody sitting Yogi fashion by the side of the road, trying to light a cigarette, a joint probably. He pulled up to a stop, dimmed his lights and got out.

He walked over slowly. As he got closer, he saw that it was a girl. She was trying unsuccessfully to light a cigarette, succeeding only in burning her fingers. She was throwing each match away and lighting another, totally absorbed in what she was doing. She did not even look around as he approached her.

He squatted beside her. "You need some help?" he said. She turned her head as if in slow motion and looked at him, her eyes like a guppy's. She was totally wasted.

"It's pretty late," he said. "And you don't look like you're in any shape to be taking care of yourself."

"Can you help me?" she said, trying to strike another match. "I drink a lot."

"Ever try to do anything about it?"

"Yeah, I did today. I went to three different places, and I told them I wanted help, but they wouldn't help me."

"Hospitals?"

"Yeah. Where they help you not to drink anymore."

"I'm sorry to hear that. Sorry they couldn't do anything for you." He shifted his weight to his other leg. "I'll do what I can. Officially, the only way I can help you is to put you under arrest. That way you'll get the care you need, through the county facilities. I'll call a car to come and get you. You read? You like to read?"

"Oh, yeah, I read a lot."

"I'm not gonna get into a big heavy thing with you about religion, but I think Jesus has an answer for you. Here." He handed her the tract. "Stick this in your pocket and read it when you feel better."

He straightened up and walked back to his car, keeping his eye on the girl. He picked up the mike and depressed the button. "One-L-twenty requesting a unit for transportation," he said. "Meet me in the alley at the rear of one-thirty-eight-fifty-five Garden Grove."

"Crazy," he thought as he drove back to the station. "These tracts are the greatest invention since the early Christians drew the sign of the fish in the sand."

"Have you thought anymore about coming out to be our beach minister?" Gary said and reached for the phone.

Steve and Nancy had come out for some "R and R." They looked at each other, then back at him. He could read nothing in their faces. Marianne was wearing an expression meant to be impenetrable, but she only succeeded in looking like a beguiling child bursting with a secret.

He dialed, still looking at them, and he hoped *his* face was impenetrable. "Fred?" he said. "Can you come over? I've got your preacher sitting right here." *Crass effrontery,* he thought, and, *Lord stop this any time, the minute I go too far.* "Fine," he said, "and bring the keys to the church."

He hung up, swung around on the bar stool and grinned a grin he did not feel. *Keep it light,* he thought. *You are caring too much. Keep it cool.*

They were still talking in generalities when Fred leaned in through the open top of the Dutch door. He was grinning and dangling some keys. Gary slid off the bar stool, and Steve got to his feet for the introductions.

"Come on," Fred said. "I'll take you down to see your new church."

There was a little cautious laughter, and a moment later they piled into two cars and headed for the big white house.

They went through it with a false boisterous enthusiasm and made exaggerated plans like young marrieds going through a sixty-thousand-dollar model home when they know that all they can afford is seventeen nine.

Back at the house they faced each other in an awkward

silence. Then Gary and Steve both spoke at once. "One step at a time," Gary began.

"Nancy is due any day," Steve was saying, and Gary motioned him to go on.

"Nancy's due. We're in no position to think about moving right now," Steve finished. They all laughed then as the absurdity of it struck them all at once.

Of course, it was ridiculous.

17

"Barrett?"

Gary looked toward the voice. It was Gillespie, a sergeant assigned to station duty.

"Yeah," Gary said. "What?"

"We've got some runaway juveniles from the placement home down on El Centro. Couple of kids, nine and ten. They've been gone since two-thirty."

Gary looked up at the clock automatically. It was 4 A.M.

"I've sent a radio car down there," Gillespie said. "Would you go down, too? You might have to set up a command post and organize a search."

Sergeants got assigned to very few types of calls. They could roll on anything they wanted to, but they got *sent* to bomb threats, missing juveniles, barricaded suspects, involved traffic accidents, things like that.

"Sure," Gary said. "Be glad to. D'you know where Randall is?"

"I'll get him," Gillespie said, getting up and starting for the door.

Gary's tanker jacket was draped over the back of his chair. He put it on and went out to his car.

Randall came loping out the door behind him, putting on his jacket. A minute later they were heading toward the same neighborhood Gary had been in a few hours earlier. The home on El Centro was only a couple of blocks from where he had been stepping carefully around pools of blood after a gang war, and where a movie producer had been shot to death in broad daylight a few weeks before.

It was an incongruous location for an orphan's home, but it had been built many years before, when the whole area had been country, wild and beautiful and unspoiled. It's as if God had blessed this little spot, Gary thought. As if, in some mysterious way, it was protected.

Unit 6A76 was waiting in front of the administration building when Gary drove up; he signaled to them and drove around to the back. The place was incredible, he thought; like an oasis in the middle of a spiritually arid desert. It was a complex of buildings set back from the street, beautifully landscaped, and fenced in with hedges. He'd been there several times. The kids who were kept there were not in trouble with the law; they were there because there were no suitable homes to place them in.

They were treated with love. The cars parked outside in the daytime had Jesus stickers and the Ichthus on their bumpers, students from Biola Seminary did volunteer work there, and the staff was right out of the top drawer. He wondered why any kid sheltered there would want to run away. Or dare to, for that matter. Any kid escaping was escaping into a caldron of filth, and was subject to anything, from getting shanghaied for a homosexual orgy to being an unwilling recruit for a porno movie.

He got out of the car and walked toward the back door. Before he could reach for the night bell, the door opened, and one of the night employees let him and Randall in. They followed him down the hall to the front office.

The night housemother was sitting there. She rose to meet them when they got to the door. The officers in the other unit were already in the room.

"Sergeant Barrett, Mrs. Seely," he said, in case she

didn't remember his name. He gave her a look that he hoped was reassuring. She indicated a chair for him and sat down again.

The officers from 6A76 prepared to leave.

"What time did you say the boys ran away, Mrs. Seely?" one of them said.

"They ran away sometime around two-thirty, between bed checks," she said. "We looked for them from then on until four, when we called you."

"Well, the broadcast has gone out with the boys' descriptions," he said. "We'll go back out and keep looking. I'm sure we'll find them soon." He nodded to Gary, and they both left.

Someone brought in coffee, and Gary questioned Mrs. Seely at length. She didn't give them much to go on. The ten-year-old had run away before, but had come back of his own accord. The nine-year-old had not given them any trouble, but his mother had promised to come and take him home that day and had called at the last minute, changing her mind. She had emotional problems, Mrs. Seely explained, and had given the boy a hard time. Gary wondered why any kid in his right mind would want to go back and live with a mother like that; the mysteries of the human psyche were hard to fathom.

At six-thirty the phone rang. Everyone tensed for a second. "It's an extension," Mrs. Seely said, and they relaxed again. "It's from the dorm," she answered, and they were silent, waiting, but she looked up almost immediately at them and announced, "They're back. They're up in the dorm."

"I'll be back," Gary said, jumping to his feet. "I'll call in the unit that's been looking for them," and he hurried on out to his car.

When he got back to the front office, the boys were

there, along with the attendant who had brought them down from the dorm.

Gary stopped short when he saw them. They were incredibly small. The shorter of the two was shivering uncontrollably.

"Mrs. Seely," Gary said, "we'd like to talk to the boys. Is that okay? And could Officer Randall take this fellow to another room?" She nodded and walked toward the door, Randall following with the taller boy. Gary was left looking down at the small—too small for a nine-year-old—waif, who had given the night staff of the placement home and several units of police officers a bad night.

"Are you scared?" he said softly. "Or cold?"

"Cold," the boy answered, and it came out in a high tremolo, expiring in a shudder that shook his small frame.

"Stand up," Gary said, peeling off his tanker jacket. The boy stood and Gary draped the jacket around him. He was lost in it, the fur collar reaching to the top of his head in back and framing his face like a halo. "That will warm you up," Gary said, sitting down again in his chair and motioning the boy to sit back down on the sofa. "What's your name?"

The boy lowered himself gingerly on the edge of the sofa and stared at the floor. "David," he answered, without raising his eyes.

"You can't take care of yourself out there in the dark, David," Gary said. "People get mugged—yes, and shot—out there in broad daylight. Grown people. Some pretty awful things could happen to a kid. This is a bad neighborhood."

David continued to stare at the floor, silent and unresponsive. "In here you're safe," Gary went on. "You're with people who love you, who care what happens to you—" He broke off suddenly, nonplussed. The kid probably had this speech memorized, he thought. All kids in here knew what went on in the neighborhood. They were old before their time, there wasn't anything you could say to them that they hadn't heard before.

"Why can't you look at me?" Gary asked, finally.

The boy hesitated so long, Gary thought he wasn't going to answer. "I can't look at anybody I talk to," he said at last, barely above a whisper.

Gary drew a deep breath to cover the pain and anger that shot through him; the wounds inflicted on a child's spirit are not the kind you can put a Band-Aid on.

"You have a great name there, David." He tried a different tack. "With a name like that, you have a lot to live up to."

Though David did not move or look up, Gary sensed a response. The boy was sending out signals, he thought, and the thought made him plunge on.

"There was a king once, named David," he said. "He was one of the greatest kings in the history of the world. He lived in ancient Israel. And when he was a boy, he watched his father's sheep. He led them across jagged cliffs and through deep gullies. The country there was really wild, but he'd find them pastureland, and water. He always seemed to know where to find it. And he'd protect them from lions and bears, too."

The boy shifted, ever so slightly, into a more comfortable position on the sofa, the stiffness going out of him almost imperceptibly.

"He killed them with a long leather sling, loaded with a stone," Gary went on. "He'd swing the sling in a circle over his head and take aim and—pfffft—the stone went through the air with deadly accuracy. He hit his mark every time. The stone had to be round and smooth, though. If it had any edges on it, he might throw a screwball and miss his mark."

The boy had stopped shivering, but he was still staring at the floor.

"Anyhow," Gary said, "one time the army of his country was fighting the army of an enemy country, and his father sent him to the battlefront to take some supplies to his older brothers. And when he got there, it turned out that these other guys, the enemy, had a giant in their army, and the king of David's country was looking for somebody brave enough to fight him. Anybody who could finish off that giant would win the war. Can you guess who decided to finish him off?"

The boy looked up at last. "David?" he said.

Gary nodded, grinning. "The big guys thought he was crazy, and his brothers called him a cocky brat. But he went to the king and got his permission, and he picked five smooth stones out of a small brook and ran toward the giant."

"And round," the boy said, staring at him now, his eyes bulging. "The stones had to be round, or he'd throw a screwball."

"Right," Gary said in surprise. "Anyhow, when the giant saw David coming at him with a leather sling, he turned purple, he was so mad. And he yelled something like 'Come over here, you *kid,* and I'll feed you to the birds.' But that was the last thing he ever said, because David twirled that sling in a circle over his head and yelled, 'The battle is God's!' and took careful aim and—pfffft—the stone flew through the air and landed smack in the middle of the giant's forehead."

The boy leaned back then, and Gary held his gaze. I've got him, he thought, and he went on quickly. "And

David, when he got to be a man, became a king. He was king of Israel, the greatest king Israel ever had. He had a lot of responsibility, as king.

"But back when he was a boy, his responsibility was to just watch his father's sheep. Maybe he didn't like it, back there alone in the rough country, but he stayed there, because he was told to. And he didn't leave until his father said he could. Your responsibility right now is to stay here until you're told you can leave. Okay?"

David nodded.

"Oh, yeah, and there's more. David got to be much more than a king." Gary waited for the boy to ask; he did not, but his look was eloquent enough. "He was one of the ancestors of Jesus. The people here have told you about Jesus. The students from Biola have, I'll bet."

The boy nodded.

"So you see, David is one of the greatest names in all the world. You have a lot to live up to, with a name like that."

The boy shifted in his seat and put up a heroic fight to keep from smiling. He lost.

"Who knows?" Gary said, "I might be sitting just a coupla feet away from a guy who is going to grow up to be a great man, one of the greatest, maybe."

The boy stared at the floor again, but this time with pleasure and embarrassment.

Randall came in then with the other boy and the housemother, and Gary stood up as she came in the room. The boy stood up too, the tank jacket slipping from his shoulders. He retrieved it and held it out to Gary, this time looking up at him.

Gary took it solemnly. "Good-bye, David," he said to the boy, with a slight emphasis on the *David*.

"Good-bye," the boy said, and he had the look of

someone who has just seen his life pass before his eyes.

As Gary drove up the Pacific Coast Highway, a picture of David, lost in the tanker jacket, stayed with him. It would be kind of wild, Gary thought, if the kid did grow up to be somebody. He pictured him on a platform, or in a press conference, saying, "A cop told me once that I had a lot to live up to with a name like David, and it was the turning point of my life." He chuckled at his own audacity, then sobered again. Why not? God was no piker. He was superextravagant, there was no limit to what He could do, and He did things big if He wanted to.

It was the next day that Steve called and said, "Nancy and I have been praying about this all week. If you're still of the same mind, we're coming."

18

When Gary announced to Fred that Steve and Nancy were coming, there was an incredulous "they *are?*" from the other end of the phone.

"Fred, this is the real thing," Gary answered. "They're coming, just like we talked about it, like we agreed on."

He waited. There was no way you could fault Fred, he thought. Fred had, materially, the most to lose. His was a hundred-thousand-dollar house. He could get twice, three times the mortgage payments if he kept it rented.

"I can't believe it's actually happening, either," Gary said, bracing himself for the fact that Fred might back out.

Fred cleared his throat. "Well, it's happening, all right," he said instead. "Praise the Lord. I'll be right down, and we'll figure out how He's going to help us swing it."

Later that night, driving to work, Gary marveled at their audacity. They had pledged money that did not exist, bracing themselves with Bible verses like "God owns the cattle on a thousand hills," and "With God *nothing* is impossible."

The first step would be the practical business of getting Steve and Nancy out there and settled in an apartment before their baby was born. But, he reminded himself, that was only the first step. He arrived at work slightly giddy at the enormousness of all the succeeding steps, as yet unknown.

He was glad that Mike, the LAPD chaplain, was going to ride with him. Mike had brought along the youth pastor from his church, a fellow by the name of Charlie Lowman.

"Hey, you called in on the right night, Mike," he said. "You're just the kind of partner I need. There's somebody I want us to go see."

They were passing the front desk when Gary heard his name. "Barrett—phone call." It was Gillespie, on desk duty. "You can take it here."

Mike and Charlie waited while Gary answered. He spoke briefly, his voice guarded. "Yeah, we'll have to get together," he finished. "Right now I'm on my way out. But I'm glad you called. Try me again."

He hung up slowly, his face thoughtful, and looked at Mike. "That was a guy I had to arrest one time," he explained.

"You don't sound happy about it," Mike said.

"It's just that I have a cop's mind," Gary said. "There's a part of me that stays cautious, no matter how much I love my fellowman."

"He wants to see you?" asked Mike.

"Yeah. And I have a gut hunch that God has something in store for him. In some strange way, he's a special person."

"If he calls again, invite him to church," Charlie said. They all chuckled at that, and headed for the door.

"Where to?" Mike said as they climbed in the car.

"Old friend of mine at UCLA Hospital, a guy by the name of Jack McCullough. He's a cop. Or he was a cop. He's retired. After he retired, his health went on the skids. He started drinking."

"What's he in the hospital now for?" Mike said.

"He's in there to die," Gary said. "He's had his last

drink. He's in intensive care now. He's had surgery." Gary paused to check a familiar-looking license plate against the hot sheet, came up with a blank. "Anyhow," he went on, "I wanted to go see him, maybe pray for him. Okay?"

They both nodded.

When they reached the hospital, Gary drove around to the Emergency Room entrance and parked. "This is the quickest way to find a patient after hours," he said.

They piled out of the car and went in. He led them past the desk and down the hall to a room that had a coffee pot and paper cups set up. "I know a lot of nurses in here," Gary said. "We'll have some coffee. Sooner or later we'll find one who will show us the way up."

They got their coffee and sat down at the only table in the large room.

"How are your plans for your church coming?" Mike said.

"We've got our pastor," Gary said, grinning.

"Hey, Sergeant Barrett!" The voice came from across the room.

"That's one of the head nurses," Gary said under his breath as he grinned at her. He was immediately embarrassed, because she headed over toward him, and at the moment he couldn't think of her name. "These are my friends," he said, and introduced her to Mike and Charlie. "And this," he went on, "is one of the best head nurses in LA."

"I'm Kelly," she said. "What are you doing here?"

"We're here to see Jack McCullough. Is it okay?"

"Sure, come on. I'm on my way back. I'll take you."

They scrambled to their feet and followed her to the door. "It'll be easier to take you than to try to tell you how to get there," she said, and plunged ahead down the hall. They put their cups down hurriedly and caught up with her.

When they came to McCullough's room, they stopped short, and Kelly opened the door. She said nothing, just smiled and motioned them in. Then she backed off, and the door swished closed behind them.

The smell of death and decay hit them like a physical blow, and they recoiled. A fresh colostomy, Gary thought, fighting nausea. McCullough lay there on his back, his eyes half-open, glazed, not blinking. Tubes were coming from him everywhere. There was an oxygen tank and the inevitable IV hanging from a pole by his bed.

Gary walked up to the head of the bed, the others following. "This is Barrett," he said, "Gary Barrett. I brought along a couple of friends. They're police chaplains."

There was no response.

"These guys would like to pray for you," he tried again.

With all the strength he had, McCullough jerked his head in assent. He tried to answer, but all that came out was a long bubbly sigh, like someone trying to call out under water. Gary went around the bed to the other side. They all put their hands on McCullough's head, and Mike began to pray. In his prayer, he laid out God's plan of salvation. "For by grace are you saved through faith; and not of yourselves: it is the gift of God: Not of works, lest any man should boast.

"All you have to do to accept Jesus into your life," Mike finished, "is give a little nod."

There was an almost imperceptible quiver of McCullough's chin. Whether or not it was meant to be a nod, Gary had the sudden conviction that McCullough had said yes to God. None of them would be able to put it into words later, but the glory of God seemed to be in the room. They stood there for a few minutes, then McCullough's eyes began to close. The staring, glazed look was gone. Gary studied him for a moment. He had not died—not yet—but he would be gone before morning.

They left the room.

"Did you feel it, too?" Gary said, after they were back in the car. And without waiting for an answer, "I just had the doggonest feeling that I'm gonna see McCullough in heaven. I think he heard us. I think he heard every word we said."

"Me too," said Mike, "I'm sure of it."

It did seem as if McCullough had come swimming up from unconsciousness just long enough to hear the Good News that God Himself had come into the world in the Person of Jesus Christ to make it very plain to man who He was, and that His Holy Spirit had come into that room on that night, to let a guy named Jack McCullough know that a relationship with God was a very personal thing.

When Gary got home, he told Marianne about McCullough, and they talked about the incredible happenings of the morning.

"There's no turning back now," Gary said. "For richer or for poorer, we've got ourselves a church." And then, "Ken Hermin called me at the station tonight. He wants us to get together."

"Gary, you've never gotten involved with an arrestee before." She said it as a statement, but it was a question.

He didn't answer.

19

The dawn straggled in, cold and sullen, shaking itself like a wet dog and sending a cold drizzle over the land.

Gary walked out on the beach at five. The gray sea was pushing whitecaps up on the sand, where they lay like piles of soapsuds, shivering, sodden, and dirty brown. They clung to the sand in clusters, as if in fright, until, tired of fighting the wind, they broke free bit by bit and went scurrying up the beach.

He stood there in his bare feet and turned his face up to the drizzle. The sea and sky melted into each other in a mist; there was no horizon. He felt the bubbly whitecaps roll up on his insteps, nibbling at him like tiny minnows in a brook. The Dobes came down and nuzzled him, then took off down the beach in great, flying leaps, oblivious to the drizzle.

I feel let down, he thought, beach people don't come out on a day like this. Aloud he said, "God, I think I'm scared." He answered himself, or God answered him, he did not know which.

"You're tired."

He realized suddenly that it was so. The excitement of the past two weeks had been fever pitch. Christians on the beach had popped up from nowhere.

"By the dozens!" Marianne had shrieked.

"One dozen," Gary had reminded her. "There are only about twelve. The great silent minority."

By ten o'clock the drizzle had stopped, but the low ground in front of the big white house was flooded.

Inside, there was the smell of fresh coffee and a wood fire, and the air of the suppressed excitement of a dozen people. It was almost more than the house could contain.

They had prayed, drunk innumerable cups of coffee, and prayed again, in that order.

"Lord, we have everything we need, except we're short a hundred and twenty-five dollars," they prayed. That came up quite often in their prayers, as if the Lord might not have heard.

At ten-fifteen they were ready.

And then people began sloshing in, taking the programs and the paper cups of coffee and finding seats. Most of them were beach people, young couples, teenagers, older people—and beaming—all of them beaming!

And the children! Gary's heart sank, and immediately he was ashamed. So many children! How could they hold a solemn church service with so many children?

At ten-thirty they began. Gary, grinning, and with a cool he did not feel, began a chorus, and before he finished the first verse, they joined in, softly at first, then louder. Parts began to emerge, and then, incredibly, a descant. By the time they went over it again, they were singing like a well-trained choir at first rehearsal. They didn't know the words, but these young people knew their music. They were born to sing!

Then Steve lifted his guitar over his head and laid it on the floor. Gary took over with a welcome, announcements, and whatever else—he never did remember—for his mind had split in two.

So many children, sitting there wide-eyed. What were they expecting? Entertainment? A magic show? By the way they were dressed, he knew that most of them had never seen the inside of a church or heard of Jesus.

What would Steve do? Be a clown? He could be, for he

had a matchless wit. Would he be the scholar? Good Lord, Gary thought with sudden panic, for he knew that Steve *was* a scholar, and a brilliant one.

He turned the service over to Steve, his grin wobbling uncontrollably, and sat down, sweating.

Steve opened his Bible and said quietly, "There are Bibles here. Raise your hand if you don't have one. Turn to the Gospel of Matthew. It's the first book in the New Testament. We're going to learn about God, and we're going to learn about Jesus. We're going to find out that Jesus *is* God; they are one and the same."

There was a rustle and hushed confusion, everyone intent on getting a Bible and finding the place, and an air of anticipation.

Then Steve began. He was a scholar, all right, but he was a teacher, in the most excellent sense of the word.

Gary became aware of something else, something strange. It was a few minutes before he could define it. There was an immense silence in the room. Except for Steve's voice, no one stirred, no one seemed to be breathing. He was scarcely aware of when the service was over.

He stirred himself, got to his feet, and began softly,

> Bless the Lord, O my soul: and all that is within me, bless his holy name.

It was a half hour before the last one went away, and only the silent minority were left. It was another ten minutes before they remembered the tithe box at the back of the room. Steve objected to passing a collection plate. The idea was to put a box in the back of the room, mention it once, and forget it. But they had forgotten to mention it.

Gary fumbled with the top of the box, shrugging in apology.

"I just forgot it," he said lamely. And he opened the top.

Money! They stared at it, unbelieving, and then stood silent while Gary counted it.

A hundred and twenty-five dollars! Including the pennies.

"I can't believe it," he said, looking up.

Sean stared at his father, wide-eyed, looking for disappointment. "That's all we asked for," he said, trying to comfort.

And the truth of his words struck them all at once. The voice of the Lord, though not audible, seemed to hang in the silence of the room.

"Why didn't you ask for more?"

20

"Hey Barrett, don't shave that beard off. We can use it. And don't change your clothes."

Gary was on his way to the locker room. He turned in the hallway and looked back. It was Cusanovich standing in the doorway of the Watch Commander's office.

"The men's restroom at the beach is the current hangout for fags. Want to go along with Rooney? He hasn't operated there before. You'll be new faces."

"Sure," Gary said.

"Just stay the way you are. You look crummy. Did you have a good time?"

"Yeah, great," Gary said. He'd been off for a month, and he'd taken Marianne and the kids to Mexico in a VW van. They'd barnstormed over the back roads, found private beaches, visited missions, stayed with poor Mexican families in tumbledown shacks and dirt-floor huts, and had come back home looking crummy and feeling great.

The assignment would be something different. And he liked Rooney, who was somewhere in his thirties, powerfully built, with blond hair and freckles that made him look much younger than he really was. He'd been in Vice for months; it would be an education with him. He was affable, good company.

Gary looked at his watch and yawned. It was 1 A.M. They had already made a couple of arrests for minor violations and gone back to the station to book their

159

arrestees and do the paperwork.

Now they were back. He was sitting in a stall, waiting. They had taken turns doing this, one in the stall, the other out by the urinals and the sinks.

There were certain rules to the game. You couldn't send out any signals, even mentally, to these guys, or make a gesture or do or say or look or even *think* anything that might be construed as entrapment.

"Want to take a break—go get some coffee?" he called out. But just then they heard someone coming. Gary heard Rooney turn on the water at one of the sinks.

The violation came surprisingly quick. Gary heard low voices, and then a scuffle. He barged out of the stall, to find Rooney grappling with a man in his late forties, who was bigger, if possible, than Rooney was. But though the man was big and powerful, Rooney was better trained and in better shape. Within seconds, he had the man facing the wall, pinned against it.

"You can't arrest me," the guy said. There was genuine fear in his voice.

"The hell I can't," said Rooney.

"You can't arrest me—for God's sake—you can't arrest me—" His voice dropped to almost a whisper. "I'm a priest." It came out halfway between a groan and a sob.

It brought Gary up with such a jolt that his mouth hung open, but Rooney was unperturbed. "So you're a priest," he said, but his voice had automatically dropped, too. And, just as automatically, he refined his terminology. "What you just did to me, sir, was an overt act. *Very* overt, see? So you're coming with us."

For most of the drive back to the station, they were silent. Rooney drove. Gary sat in the back with the arrestee. He studied the man who sat, his head down, breathing deeply and letting the air out with great shuddering sighs in an effort to control himself.

"Sir," Gary said finally, "I know that sin is sin, but if you had to do something like this, wouldn't a clandestine meeting in a motel room with a woman have been a better way to go?"

He realized immediately he had said something that not only made no sense morally, but was outright stupid. He was surprised that such specious reasoning had even entered his mind. But he was even more shocked at the fact that the man was genuinely horrified.

He lifted his head sideways and looked at Gary long enough to say, "*What?* And indulge in sexual intercourse outside of wedlock?"

Gary was too astonished to pursue the subject. "What's the name of your monsignor?" he asked.

The man gave it. Gary fished for his notebook and wrote it down. "And his address and phone number, sir?" The man gave them in a voice of resignation and resumed his deep breathing.

Back at the station, Rooney took him into one of the interrogation rooms. Gary went into the Watch Commander's office and dialed the number. It was 2 A.M.

They left the man in a detention room and went down the hall to get some coffee.

It was 3 A.M. before the monsignor showed up. He was a wizened little man, very sincere, very concerned. He had obviously dressed in a great hurry. Gary was sorry for him.

"Won't you sit down, sir?" he said politely and pulled up a chair. The monsignor sank into it wearily. He asked the nature of the arrest, where it had taken place, and the details. He had been through this before.

"We won't book him, sir," Gary said when he had

finished. "We will release him to your custody."

"Yes. Of course," the monsignor said. "He will get counseling. We have retreats. We have ways of dealing with this sort of thing. We try to help these troubled men." He sighed. "You're not Catholic," he said. It was a statement, more than a question.

Gary shook his head.

"Tell me," the monsignor went on. "What do you do with your religious leaders when they fall?"

It was a totally unexpected question, and Gary was taken aback for a moment. He looked at the man, trying to discern sarcasm, but there was none.

"Nothing, I guess," he said. "Not that I know of. We ignore them, or shut up to try to protect them, though I wonder now that you've asked me this, if we are not really trying to protect ourselves. Anyhow, I guess we just, in the end, toss them off."

There was a silence for a moment. Then, "I already knew that," the monsignor said. "I just wondered if you did."

Gary nodded.

Then, "What is your religion?" the monsignor said unexpectedly.

Gary hesitated for a moment. Religion? "Actually, I'm very turned off by religion," he said. "But I am terribly excited about the power of the living God in people's lives."

"Ah," the monsignor said, and then sank into silence again. "You have gay churches right here in Los Angeles," he said finally. "In the Protestant religion."

"That's what I mean about religion turning me off," Gary said. "A way of life is one thing, even if it's church oriented. A total commitment to Jesus Christ is another."

The monsignor nodded his understanding, and Gary went on. "I go to a little church on the beach," he said. "We started with only three couples. We have a pastor who really feeds us the Word of God. We've had healings, miraculous healings. We've had people delivered from dope and alcohol, we've seen lives turned around. Things are *happening*." He stopped, embarrassed, realizing he was talking to a Catholic monsignor. There was a brief silence.

Then, "Ah yes," the monsignor said softly. "There is a resurgence of the Holy Spirit of God in the Catholic Church, and we have seen miracles, too. And a great hunger for the Word of God. I know what you mean." He smiled suddenly. "I think, Sergeant Barrett," he said, rising, "that God's Holy Spirit is moving in the world today, and He doesn't care about denominations. He cares only about believers."

He extended his hand. It was small and dry, but his grip was firm. A few minutes later, Gary watched the two of them disappear down the hall toward the front door, the taller man's head bent.

"That gave me a jolt I'm going to remember for days," he said later to Rooney over coffee. "I'm not naive, and I think I've seen everything, but somehow this just totally throws me."

"It's four o'clock, Rooney said. "Are you ready to go home?"

"Yeah, in a minute. There's something I want to get from my locker first."

He went back to the locker room and got the card he had been writing for Marianne while he was waiting for Rooney at the beginning of watch. He'd bought it on his way to work. This would have been Melissa's birthday, had she lived. The card was a night view of the ocean: a pale moon, a silvery path across the gray calm waters, one low sea gull sending his cry into the silent night.

Inside he had written, "I thought of addressing this to Melissa, but even though this card is for her, I give it to you."

The message on the card was:

> Sometimes in the silent night
> The thought of you is a tender light . . . .

21

The change of watch at the precinct was not the first time Gary had seen a beaten child; he had seen many, too many of them. But it was the first time he had ever been angry with God. It was nearly a year now since that first church service, and during that time, he had never lost a sense of wonder and praise.

Gary came out of the station to handle the change of watch (a dubious honor assigned to sergeants), and shivered a little. It had been a warm day, but the evening chill had set in early, and now, at midnight, it was downright cold.

When the unit pulled up to the gas pumps, he didn't realize the officers had a passenger until they opened the back door and a child climbed out. A boy about five, he guessed, dressed in what had once been a good matched outfit, but now it was torn half off, and his shoes were missing.

"Who's your partner?" he asked the officers, grinning at the boy.

"We got him down at the beach, Sarge," they said.

"Runaway? Or lost?"

"Neither."

The boy looked up, and in the glare of headlights, Gary saw his face. It was puffed and caked with blood. His eyes were swollen nearly shut, his hair matted and bloody.

Gary looked over the child's head at the two officers.

"You should see the rest of him," one of them said,

and then to his partner, "Fill him in. This kid's got to go to the bathroom." And he swooped the child up in his arms and headed for the station.

"Sarge, it's the darndest thing you ever saw," the other officer said. "This little guy was taken down to the beach by his father."

"Who beat him up?"

"His *father*. Near as we can figure at this point, his father beat him up and left him at the beach this afternoon. He's been wandering around the beach all afternoon and all night, till we got him at a gay bar."

"You found him in a gay bar?"

"He finally wandered into one of the gay bars down there on West Channel Road, looking for help. They called us, and we went over and picked him up."

"Could the boy tell you anything more?"

"The father had been fighting with the mother and took it out on the kid. He did this to him, then just dumped him on the beach and abandoned him."

"Jesus," Gary said softly.

"Yeah," the officer said and let out a few expletives. Gary did not correct him, but his remark had not been an expletive, it had been a cry from his heart.

"Okay," he said finally, "I'll be in in a few minutes, soon's I finish the watch change."

"Oh," the officer said over his shoulder as he turned to go, "the boy's father is a doctor."

Gary could not answer. He was stunned. He finished the watch change in silence, a slow anger growing inside him. "Jesus," he kept saying to himself, and over and over, "Jesus."

Back inside the station, there was an attempt at double-checking, but they could get no more than they already had. The father was a doctor of some kind, as nearly as they could figure out, a psychiatrist or psychologist. The child was exhausted. Gary left him with the officers who brought him in, and the last he saw of him, he was asleep, his head limp on the shoulder of the big cop who was carrying him down the hall to a cot.

Back outside the station, Gary breathed deeply in the chill air, but the pressure and heaviness inside him were still there, and the anger. He trotted over to where his car was waiting. He pulled out of the driveway and into the traffic, the radio squawking its endless string of code numbers. The tour of field duty was beginning.

Tomorrow was Sunday.

The first thing you did was turn off your feelings.

Sunday morning he drove up the Pacific Coast Highway in a depression so deep it was physical. His chest felt constricted, his throat tight, his stomach knotted and heavy.

To his left, the Pacific was sparkling blue, the whitecaps frothy and snowy white, and the beaches were white and sun swept and clean. God's world looked pure and innocent, with an almost pristine beauty. But if you got close, he thought bitterly, if you got close, you'd see that the sea is really gray and the sand is littered with discarded cans and bottles and dotted with tar.

He tried to think of something good, dredged his memory for some Scripture, came up finally with, "All things work together for good to them that love God," but it ended with a roar of fury. He tightened his grip on the steering wheel and bellowed like an angry bull, until his car was filled with the sound. It ricocheted off the sides and resounded in his ears.

After church he and Marianne had dinner out with Steve and Nancy. Their table looked out over the marina, with its myriad of sailboats bobbing in their slips.

"Why does God let these things happen?" Gary asked, when he had told them about the boy. "Why?"

Steve hesitated a minute. "I'm going to give you what you'll think is a typical theological answer," he said. "But it's man's separation from God that has brought about such things."

"Don't give me a typical theological answer," Gary said. "Not right now." His eyes were pleading.

"When Adam sinned, the human race sinned; when Adam fell, the human race fell. And we all suffer for it—corporately."

Gary sighed impatiently. "It doesn't answer the cry in my heart," he said.

"Nor in mine," Steve said. "But we have Western minds. We think in terms of individualism. The Eastern mind never thought that way, nor does it now. The Eastern mind thinks corporately. And whether or not we like it, we are still living in terms of corporate responsibility in God's eyes."

"It doesn't make sense," Gary said stubbornly. "I know you're right, but it still doesn't make sense to my *feelings*. It seems irrational to me."

"The realm of God is not rational or irrational," Steve said. "It's *transrational*. It's beyond anything we can figure out. There are some questions we simply can't answer."

"I'm not arguing with you, Steve," Gary said. "I'm trying to accept it. But if you could have seen that kid . . . ."

"Well, one good thing has come of it," Nancy interrupted. "We'll all think of him and pray for him now, and maybe he'd never have been held up to God if this hadn't happened."

They nodded, silent.

"And remember," Steve said as they rose to leave, "we are receiving *benefits* corporately, as well as the responsibilities. All of us receive the corporate benefits, whether or not we deserve them. The rain falls on the fields of the guy who hates God, just as it does on the fields of the Christian farmer up the road."

"I know it," Gary said, trying to sound convincing.

Out by the car, Steve took up where he had left off. "Look at what's happened to us," he persisted. "To Nancy and me. Our daughter was born safely, and God has blessed our ministry."

Yes, Gary thought grimly, *and Nancy has developed multiple sclerosis*. He resisted the impulse to glance in her direction. He was trying hard to get what Steve was saying, he knew Steve was right, but everything was coming up negative in his mind.

"And look what's happened to the church," Steve went on.

"Yeah," Gary said. He remembered the prayers, the work, and yes, the problems. They had been forced to vacate the big white house because of complaints from disgruntled neighbors. Before they had finished reeling from the blow, they had prayed themselves into leasing the school down the road on Sundays. And their meager congregation had grown to three hundred.

He managed a guilty grin. "I know it," he said. "I know it. But I just can't *feel* it. My mind keeps getting in the way."

They parted then, and Steve and Nancy started for their own car.

"Remember now, I'm going to pray for that little boy," Nancy called back, and she put her hand on a car fender to keep her balance, and she was *smiling*.

Gary watched them walk away, Steve's arm around her, then he turned to Marianne. "Everything keeps coming up negative in my mind," he voiced his thought, "I can't seem to help it."

That night he walked the Dobes on the beach, alone. Marianne had sensed his need to be alone and did not offer to go along.

"I'm having a hard time with this, Lord," he said aloud, as he walked along in the dark. "I know what Steve said is right. But I feel like the guy in the Bible when he said to Jesus, 'Lord, I believe, help my unbelief.' "

There was no moon. The fog was rolling in, clinging close to the ground, and the dogs seemed to be floating on it as they skimmed along, only their heads and the tops of their backs showing.

"Help my unbelief," he said again. "I can't handle this, Lord. I just can't handle this, take care of my anger."

He walked on for a moment and then stepped on a stone and stopped. He looked down, at the fog curling around his knees. He could not see his feet. He sat down suddenly, the fog now up to his ears, and the dogs came back and licked his face as he stared into the dark.

22

"Don't bring your street language home!" Marianne's eyes were blazing.

"I had a bloody night!" Gary shot back, and realized he was shouting.

"You always have a bloody night on Saturday!" she said.

This was going to be one of the bitterest of what was getting to be an impressive history of Sunday-morning quarrels. And as usual, she was going to have the last word.

But Sean did. "Cops are always mean sometimes," he said to Mike from the bedroom. "They have to be."

"All cops are not mean," Gary said from the hall "Only *some* of them *some* of the time. And I've got news for you. There are *some* mean missionaries, too. And *some* mean doctors. And *some* mean ministers."

"Why?" Sean stuck his head out of the bedroom door. "Why should missionaries and ministers be mean ever?"

"Because they're human!" Gary said, and now his anger was turning on himself. Good grief, he was fighting like a kid.

He slammed into the bathroom, got his shaving gear ready, and stared morosely at himself in the mirror. Might be a good idea, he thought, if he shaved off his moustache. He decided it did make him look mean. If you looked mean, you acted mean. He began to lather his face. Marianne didn't have a moustache, and she was mean, he thought irrelevantly. He started to chuckle, checked it. This was no time to be funny. If he didn't stay

171

mad, Marianne would win the argument. He decided to leave the moustache on.

It was while he was drying himself after his shower that he made up his mind to go back out there and be a martyr. And as one of the exigencies of martyrdom was that one should remain absolutely innocent, he decided that Marianne was wrong to start a fight just after he'd had a bloody night and just before he was about to go down to church and lead the worship service. He'd forgive her, he thought.

It occurred to him that these Sunday-morning battles were of a different ilk than all the others. They had a dimension that was lacking in their weekday disagreements, which were pallid in comparison. There was an element of hate in them, the desire to hurt, to draw blood, something almost fiendish. And his language always seemed to deteriorate on Sunday mornings.

He stopped, his arm halfway into his robe sleeve, then finished the job, tying his robe around him in slow motion, as the revelation came full-blown. They were Satan's Sunday stakeouts, and he'd been walking right into them, like a bungling amateur. Satan's just waiting for Sunday morning to come along, he thought, so he can nail me. Gary had learned his tactical know-how as a cop. Why didn't he know it as a Christian?

Paul had thundered in his letter to the Ephesians, that *we're not fighting against people made of flesh and blood; we're fighting against people without bodies—the evil rulers of the unseen world, mighty satanic beings and huge numbers of wicked spirits.*

If the Christian life was a spiritual warfare, why didn't he get in the fight? James had written, "Resist the devil, and he will flee from you," and he meant *cry out!*

"All right, Lord," Gary said aloud, "I'm crying out

right now. I can't do this on my own. I'm taking a stand against Satan right now, but I'm taking it in *Your strength.*"

He stood there for a minute, feeling nothing. Then he felt two things at once: a peace he wouldn't have dreamed possible ten minutes earlier, and an eagerness to go make it right with Marianne.

He passed her in the hall on his way to the bedroom to dress. It was incredibly easy. He took her by the shoulders. "I'm sorry, Stacy," he said softly. "Can you forgive me?"

"*I'm* sorry," she said. "You worked all night, and you've got to go back again this afternoon. I wasn't thinking. I just went bonkers."

"I've got to get down there and get my music ready," he said, not at all surprised. He'd already known back in the bathroom that the battle was won.

"Will you come right back and go to bed?" she said, and kissed him on the cheek.

"Yup," he said. "As soon as I finish the music."

If he weren't an elder and Marianne weren't the unofficial Christian education director, they'd probably have an easier time being spiritual, he thought as he drove down to the church.

He wondered again about being filled with the Holy Spirit. Marianne had certainly been touched by God in some way that could not be explained in human terms. Since that night at Chuck Smith's church, she had a hunger for God's Word and a zeal that she had never even approached before. And she still had it, after years. It might wane occasionally, but it always came back. She never made any great claims for her spirituality; he wondered about people who did. If one were to believe them, they never got angry, only righteously indignant, never got discouraged, never made mistakes.

The only change in himself, he thought, was a new and uncomfortable awareness of his shortcomings, especially his temper, and a tender conscience that gave him no end of trouble. He had been a lot more comfortable, he decided, before he had purposed to know a closer walk with Jesus.

"I still have trouble with my mouth, Lord," he said under his breath, just before he walked into the churc .

Back at the house, Sean was confronting Marianne. "Mother, why does Dad call you Stacy sometimes?" he asked.

She looked at him a moment, and her eyes were soft. "When Dad calls me Stacy," she said, "he means 'I love you.' "

"But what does the name *Stacy* mean?" he persisted.

"That," she said, "is what I won't tell anybody."

Gary was not too far into the watch when the call came. "Ambulance traffic, juvenile pedestrian involved." It came out of the little speaker under the dashboard in an impersonal monotone.

It sounded like a mess. They would need traffic control for this one. He decided to roll by and see if he could help. He made a U-turn and headed toward the scene.

It turned out to be a street lined with parked cars. The traffic was already piling up. He pulled up alongside a parked car, got out quickly, and ran toward the small form sprawled in the street. It was a little girl, lying in a pool of her own blood. As he squatted beside her, he heard the paramedics pull up behind, killing their siren, and then the slamming of the ambulance doors.

He eased his hand gently under her head. Her hair was sticky with blood. He took a carotid pulse. It fluttered wildly, fibrillating under his touch, and then lay still and her body relaxed. And while the paramedics were taking over and while he still held her, she died.

He looked up at the people who were standing by, silent. It wasn't hard to pick out the child's parents, their faces naked, stripped of all expression, sagging with shock.

He shook his head negative, steeling himself against the cries he knew would come. He eased his hand out from under the child's head and straightened up and started toward them and his sense of helplessness was so great that it smothered him.

"Sergeant," someone said, and he turned to see a priest getting out of a car a few feet away.

"I'm glad you're here," Gary said in undertones. "The child is dead. The parents are right behind me."

The priest looked beyond Gary, first at the child and then at the parents. "My God," he said, "I know this family. I christened this child." In a moment he was beside them, his arms around them, the tears streaming down his own face, sharing their agony. *Weep with them who weep,* Gary thought, *that's what Jesus did.*

He put it resolutely in the back of his mind for the rest of his watch.

Back at the station, he went to the coffee machine, fishing in his pocket for coins and fighting off rising anger.

Then he realized an officer was standing there with a cup of coffee in his hand. Gary had never seen him before. "Hi," he said automatically, "I'm Barrett. Gary Barrett."

"Hi, Sergeant Barrett," the officer said. "I'm Lopez. Nash Lopez. I'm a rookie."

I could have told you that by the new lint on your suit,

Gary thought. But he remembered when he was one, and said instead, "How're things going?"

Lopez just shrugged. "The biggest jolt I've had so far," he said, "was when I found out how much people hated cops."

Gary tested his coffee to see if it was cool enough. "I know," he said. "When your neighbors find out you're a cop, they're incredulous. They look at you in your slacks and T-shirt, working in your garden, and they can't believe it; you know, you're the guy down the street, how can you be a cop. It's weird."

Lopez nodded.

"Even the nicest people have an aversion to cops," Gary said, warming to his subject. "We're suddenly the enemy when we confront them with authority."

"Nobody likes authority in somebody else," Lopez said.

"We have a congenital aversion to authority," Gary said. "We're born with it."

He fished for some more coins, got himself another cup of coffee. "There was a guy who lived up the street from me," he said. "We weren't close friends, but we were friendly whenever we saw each other. Then one night he was at a party across the street, and somehow it came up that I was a cop. He was so mad, he came tearing across the street to my house and ripped my front gate off."

"You're kidding."

Gary laughed. "No, I'm not. He tore the gate off and then he got into the garage and started tearing that apart. We heard him out there cussing and telling the world how he hated cops, and we went out and told him to knock it off and go home. He was just drunk."

"He went home?"

"He left our garage, that's all I know. When all his inhibitions were gone, this hatred of authority came pouring out. Actually, he was a nice guy."

"How'd he act after that?"

"Great," Gary said. "He didn't even remember he'd done it the next day. We just never brought it up again."

"I stopped a woman the other night, pulled her over because she didn't have a rear license plate," Lopez said. "It turned out she had it on the front seat alongside her. It had come off and she was planning to get it put back on next morning. But she bit my head off. She wanted to know why the police didn't go out and chase criminals, instead of wasting the taxpayers' money bothering honest people."

"What did you say? If you hadn't stopped her, you'd have been delinquent."

"Yeah, but it didn't seem important," Lopez said. "I just tipped my hat and gave her my best LAPD smile and let her go. But when she drives away she's got Jesus stickers on her car."

"That's what I mean," Gary said. "Even the nicest people, when they're taken by surprise, can show this rebellion against authority; it's almost an atavistic reaction. We got it from Adam."

"I can't wait to get into some real heavy action," Lopez said.

Gary checked his watch, gulped down the last of his coffee. "Well, end of watch," he said. "I'm going home."

"Great talking to you, Sergeant Barrett," Lopez said.

"Good talking to you, Nash," Gary said. "And when you get into the heavy stuff, remember you're a cop, but don't forget you're a human being, okay?"

"Okay."

The moon was bright on the water, highlighting the whitecaps tumbling in toward the shore, as Gary drove up the Pacific Coast Highway. He thought about the immutability of God and the clocklike precision of the tides and the infallible seventh wave, which always came in bigger than all the others in a seven-wave set. He wondered if the great seventh ever failed, ever missed.

And then he realized he could no longer see the road. He was crying, and he did not even know when he had started or what he was crying about. He started to look for a place to turn off. He found one, just past Point Mugu. He pulled off the road, and killed the engine.

The child who had died in his arms, whom he had so resolutely put out of his mind, had been there all the time. She had been there even while he had been talking with Nash—such small talk, such drivel. He put his head down on the steering wheel, his throat aching. He cried without sound, just swallowing hard. His tears burned his face and dropped down on his thighs.

He thought of Michelle and her fawnlike eyes. He'd have to take her fishing. He'd take her fishing on his next day off, and this time leave the boys home. He suddenly longed to do something for her to let her know that she was special. The dead child had been so beautiful, her death so senseless. He could still feel her fluttering pulse beneath the pressure of his fingers. He cried until he was spent.

He pulled up in front of his house, got out of the car, and let himself in, his throat still aching; the tears had brought no relief. It was 4 A.M. He turned on the light and went upstairs. Marianne was sleeping. He bent over and kissed her. Her breath was soft, like babies' fingers.

All the horrors of this or any other night could be dispelled, he thought, at just the touch of her.

"Marianne," he said softly, and then again, "Marianne." She awakened reluctantly, and he said again, "Marianne."

Then she was wide awake at the urgency in his voice. "What's wrong?" she said.

"Can you come downstairs for a few minutes?" he said. He left while she was still fumbling for her robe.

He went downstairs and into Michelle's room. He peeled the covers off her and picked her up and carried her into the boys' room. He woke them up, then sat on the floor, propped against Mike's bed, Michelle still in his arms. They got up sleepily and crawled up beside him and propped themselves up against him. Marianne came in and without a word curled up on the floor alongside him, too.

He held them all, caressing them and attempting awkwardly a rocking motion, as if he would rock them like babies.

"A little girl, just like you, Michelle, got hit by a car yesterday," he said at last. "And she died in my arms." He swallowed hard. "I felt her pulse, and while I was feeling it, it fluttered and then it was still."

They were all silent; the children did not ask any of the curious and unwittingly callous questions children might ask.

"She was so beautiful, like Michelle," he said at last. He just held them then, in silence, until the children were asleep again and he and Marianne got them back in bed and went upstairs.

"Thanks for coming downstairs," he said, and that was all he said, he was too exhausted to say any more.

23

Gary came up from the marina, a string of huge fish in his hand, Michelle bouncing ahead of him excitedly. It was Sunday morning, but it was also his first day off since he had vowed to take her fishing alone; he had gotten up at five in order to do it.

Marianne was outside the door, waiting for them. "I thought you might be late for church," she called. "You had me worried." And then, "Wow!" when she saw the fish.

"Do you think we can have them for dinner?" he said.

"Sure," she said. "You can fillet some of them after church."

He put them down on the driveway, hosed off his hands. "You can put them in that tub of water for now, Michelle," he said. "After church I'll teach you how to fillet a fish. Right now I've got to go down and get my music started." He hurried off to get ready.

The service was on the beach; they held it there every few weeks. People came with beach towels and blankets and sprawled, and strangers who had come to the beach from town sat around the periphery, curious and respectful.

After church was over, Gary and Marianne lingered, reluctant to leave.

We're going home and filleting fish," Marianne said finally. "Aren't you, Gary?"

But Gary didn't answer. He was looking past her, down the beach. She followed his gaze. There was a man, a young man, coming toward them in a slow, loping jog. He had semilong hair and beard, and he was dressed in jeans and boots, and what looked like, even from a distance, a very expensive shirt. He kept coming, digging the toes of his boots in the sand, letting his long arms swing loosely and easily.

"It looks like Hermin," Gary said.

The muscles in his buttocks and legs tightened automatically in a move to get to his feet. But the cop in his brain gave no orders for them to complete the move. He froze at that point for a moment before he was hardly aware of it. Then he scrambled to his feet. "Ken," he called, "Ken Hermin! We're over here!"

Marianne scrambled to her feet, too. Hermin waved, and kept up his loping gait, not slowing his pace until he got close. Then he stopped, suddenly shy. Or had he felt the same hesitation?

Marianne was the first to speak. "Hi!" she said. "So you came at last. We're glad."

Gary put his arm around Marianne's waist. "Marianne, this is Ken Hermin, which you already knew. And Ken, this is Marianne, my wife."

"Hi, Marianne," Ken said, then suddenly nobody knew what to say. "I meant to get here in time for church," Ken said finally. "I had an awful time finding you. I knew you lived somewhere around this beach. I asked at the deli. They told me you'd be down here."

"Come on up to the house, Ken," Gary said, almost too heartily. "We're going to have some of the freshest fish you ever tasted. Just caught them this morning."

Ken hesitated only a moment. "Yeah, great. I'd like to," he said.

"Where's your car?" Gary asked.

"I don't have one," Hermin said. "I hitchhiked."

They started up the beach toward the road. When they reached the little Datsun, Ken stopped. "Hey, just tell me where you live and I'll walk down. I don't want to crowd you out."

"What do you mean?" Gary asked.

"Didn't you say you had three children?"

"Oh, they've got their bikes," Gary said, his hand on the door handle, but he paused imperceptibly. He hoped that Ken hadn't noticed. "D'you mind climbing in back, Ken? And watch it, the seat's broken."

They scrambled in, Marianne in the front, and headed for the house. When they pulled up in front of the house, the children were already there, parking their bikes.

"We've got company," Gary called as they got out of the car. "For dinner."

The children came over expectantly. Gary introduced them.

"Are you going to eat my fish?" Michelle asked, her eyes dancing. She ran ahead of them, over to the driveway where the fish were in the tub.

"Sure he is," Gary said. "We're going to teach you how to fillet a fish. Ken is good at it."

Gary set up a bench and went into the garage to get the filleting knives. For a moment, only a flash, his brain sent no message to his muscles, and he hesitated.

My cop's brain, he thought. His reflexes were taking over again. He took the knives and went back out and handed one to Michelle, and they began the business of filleting the fish, the boys standing by respectfully. The rule of the house was that one did not fillet anyone else's fish. This was Michelle's day. They set about the task seriously, like a team of surgeons, Gary and Ken instructing Michelle, who from long watching, turned out to be an expert.

Marianne called from the house for the boys to come in and set the table.

"Who is he?" they wanted to know.

"He's just a friend of Dad's," she said. It was better if they did not know. She had spent sleepless nights praying for this man. He had never really been entirely out of her mind.

· Dinner was a jovial one, Marianne's salad a masterpiece.

"Boy is this ever good," Ken said. "This salad is terrific."

"Come back sometime, Ken," Marianne said. "I'll make you some vegetable soup."

"Gee, I'd like that," Ken said. "I'd sure like that. I hope you'll let me."

"Yeah," Gary said noncommittally.

After the dishes were stacked, they sat around the living room. Ken chose the hearth, which unwittingly made him the central figure, them the audience. He sat on it, his hands on his spread knees.

"Tell us, Ken," Gary said. "How've you been doing? We've been anxious about you."

"Oh, I've been knocking around. I haven't been doing too well," Ken said. "I did make an album."

"You did? That's great. How did you make out?"

"Didn't sell too well. Of course, I was hoping it would be a gold record. It just kinda pooped out. And then I've been backpacking. Went up in the Sierras with another guy."

"What about Edith?"

Ken shrugged. "She got married. It wasn't the real thing. There's nobody right now." And he went back to his account of the backpacking trip in great detail.

Gary listened, nodding at the proper times, but his

mind was split in two. A thin wisp of apprehension was curling up his spine like smoke. He was looking at Ken without seeing him. He was seeing, in his mind, only the mail slot and hearing Ken's voice behind it. *I'm watching that mail slot real close, and if anyone comes in here, you've got a dead hostage on your hands. You're so covered that it's sickening, Buster.*

He knew then why his hand had paused on the door handle of the Datsun when Ken had said, *I thought you told me you had three children.*

He looked at Marianne surreptitiously. She was listening, apparently without any fear at all. *Ken had a hostage then, he's got hostages now. My own family. In my own house.*

The account of the backpacking petered out. Gary had hardly heard a word of it.

"What about your Uncle Charley?" he asked.

"Oh," Ken stopped short for a minute. "He's still mad at me for what I did. We aren't speaking."

"I'm sorry to hear that," Gary said. "Your Uncle Charley will come around. Give him time." *What have I done? I've invited this man into my home. I've broken all the rules of safety.*

The words of Judd's report came back. *Barrett, disregarding all personal safety, exposed himself to the suspect* . . . .

And now he had disregarded all the rules of safety, only this time he had exposed his family. He thought of his gun, hidden away safely upstairs. What good would it do him now?

"Okay," he said with a calm he did not feel. "Forget the past. What are you going to do from here on out? You've got a whole life ahead of you, Ken."

Did Ken really come alone? He said he'd hitchhiked.

Did he have an accomplice with a car? A gun?

"These backpacking trips are great," Ken was saying. "I'd like to go again. I wish you'd go with me."

"Sounds great," Gary said vaguely, but he didn't pursue it and there was a silence.

Then, "Well, so the album wasn't such a smash," Ken said. "I can make another one. I'm not finished yet."

Gary was about to answer when Michelle got up to change her seat, walking past the hearth in front of Ken. Ken swooped her in his arms, sat her on his lap, and she curled up against him. The thin thread of apprehension turned to fear.

He heard it again as if he were there: *Do not open that mail slot or this gal is dead, this gal is real dead.* He felt the sweat running from his hair, down his neck.

He shot a quick glance at Marianne, and then he knew. She had been thinking what he had been thinking all along.

And then the Dobermans barked.

"We have more members to our family," he grinned, but his grin was wobbly. "I'll let them in."

He went to the back door and opened it. They came with leaping bounds and went up to Ken, their stubby tails wagging frantically. Ken stretched out his free arm to them, leaned forward to nuzzle them, and they nuzzled him joyfully, ecstatically, as he murmured terms of endearment to them.

Gary watched, remembering that morning so long ago, but this time he remembered that Ken had said, *Hey, Barrett, you told me you were going to pray for me.* And they had prayed together, their fingers locked. His cop's mind stirred again, but feebly this time, and then went on automatic pilot.

"I'm not finished yet," Ken was saying, stroking the

dogs. "But I'm not all straightened out yet, either."

Gary opened his mouth to speak, but Marianne took the words out of his mouth. "Jesus is the answer to your problems, Ken," she said. "You've tried everything else. You haven't tried Him yet."

"I know, I know," Ken said. "But I'll get my head on straight. I'm going to a psychiatrist. Twice a week."

"That's great as far as it goes," she said. "But it just doesn't go far enough. You need to give your life to Christ. You need to be completely turned around, born again."

Gary's mind began to function on two levels. On one level he was listening to their conversation. On the other level he went off on a tangential spree. He remembered the promises he had made to God when he had been on his way to confront Ken.

I give my life to You, no matter how this turns out, he had said. Then he realized he was not now looking at Ken Hermin. He had come full circle. He was face-to-face with his own commitment.

"I have to get going," Ken was saying. "I have to get a ride before dark." He gave Michelle a quick squeeze and let her slide off his lap. The dogs had been asleep at his feet, but as he got up, they got up too, their stubby tails wagging.

"Can I take you to a bus?" Gary asked.

"No, it's a cinch to get a ride back from the beach at this hour," Ken said. "Everybody's going home, and a lot of them are surfers. I identify with surfers." He made for the door.

The good-byes were said. Then Gary and Ken stood in the doorway, facing each other. Gary remembered when he had put his hands on either side of Ken's face and looked into empty, vapid eyes. Now the eyes were warm and shy, and something else. They were pleading.

"I'd like to go backpacking with you, Ken," Gary said, and suddenly he realized that he meant it, that Ken was a friend he wanted to see again.

"You mean that?"

"I mean that. Call us. Call us soon. We don't want to lose track of you." He raised his hands toward Ken's face the way he had done that morning so long ago, but he put his hands on Ken's shoulders instead. "Remember what we've told you about Jesus," he said, "and promise you'll phone us, okay?"

"Hey Dad—Mom!" Mike cried, sticking his head through the open top of the Dutch door. "The sea is phosphorescent. Come on out!" He disappeared, running.

Gary and Marianne walked down to the beach. It was dark now, and the sea was alive with phosphorescent fire, reflected in the moonlight. The children were leaping into the waves, coming up with their arms over their heads, the sparkles following them, shooting in all directions.

"It's like the fairy in the Disneyland films," Sean had once said. "She flits across the TV screen waving her wand and shoots sparkles all over the place."

And it was true. The phosphorescent sea had turned them into sparkling figures, on fire in the night.

Gary walked slowly, Marianne beside him. Oh, God, he thought, for all these years—how many years—I've wanted to be filled with the Holy Spirit. Now I believe I was filled way back then, when I first asked. With me it was just more quiet, it was a growing awareness of my own shortcomings, a growing desire to be closer to You. It just didn't happen to me the way I wanted it to. I expected to be perfect, and when I wasn't, I thought I didn't have it.

"I think I'm a late bloomer," he said aloud. "Every time I think I have God all figured out, He does something that, to me, seems totally irrational."

"Here comes ole Dad, with the speed of light!" Sean shrieked from the water, and ducked into a wave, leaving sparks behind him.

"Come on in, Dad!" Mike and Michelle shouted.

Gary sprinted toward the water, more to please them than because he wanted to, and did a broad jump, landing on his bottom in the shallow water, his heels ploughing furrows in the wet sand. He scrambled to his feet, went in deeper, with long strides, and leapt into the air the way the children had done, going down in a sitting position, his arms upraised. Their shrieks faded as he went under and sank to the bottom.

He felt the bubbles against his nose.

It was quiet.

All the apprehension and tension of the afternoon was gone.

He was inundated with joy.

On the way back to the house, they were silent, spent, shivering in their beach towels.

Gary reached for Marianne's hand. "I love you, Stacy," he said.

The children's heads came up like pointers'. They looked toward their mother. But they knew without asking that she would never tell them what it meant.